W9-BXY-696

Forks in the Road

Editor: Mike Beno
Contributing Editor: Clancy Strock
Assistant Editors: Jean Steiner, John Schroeder,
Bettina Miller, Mike Martin
Art Director: Linda Dzik
Production Assistants: Claudia Wardius, Ellen Lloyd
Photo Coordination: Trudi Bellin, Mary Ann Koebernik
Editorial Assistants: Joy Snyder, Blanche Comiskey,
Jack Kertzman
Publisher: Roy J. Reiman

© 1998 Reiman Publications, L.P.
5400 S. 60th St., Greendale WI 53129

Reminisce Books

International Standard Book Number: 0-89821-217-0
Library of Congress Card Catalog Number: 97-75525
All Rights Reserved
Printed in U.S.A.
Cover Photo by Darryl R. Beers

For additional copies of this book or information on
other books, write: Reminisce Books, P.O. Box 990,
Greendale WI 53129.

Credit card orders call toll-free: 1-800/558-1013.

Contents

Introduction

By Clancy Strock
Contributing Editor
Reminisce Magazine

THE ISN'T a person among us who can't point to at least one event, accident, whim or decision that changed their life forever.

That's what the personal stories in this book are all about. They were shared by the readers of *Reminisce*, North America's most popular nostalgia magazine.

In a recent issue, we asked readers to send us these interesting and often amazing stories, and I predict they'll set you to pondering the mysterious unseen forces and events that shaped your own life.

Some people call it fate. Others say it's destiny, the work of Divine Providence or a fork in the road of life.

Looking back over my own 74 years, I realize I was one of those hapless souls who never had a master plan to roadmap his life. As a result, I took more forks in my highway of living than all the backroads in the Kentucky mountains.

I came to my first fork in the road in 1939, when I was 15. A teacher took me aside and suggested I give serious thought to becoming a journalist.

He'd Rather Play Music

At the time, I had a vague ambition to become a professional musician. Maybe I'd play trumpet in one of those dance bands that graced the Aragon, Trianon or Edgewater Beach Hotel ballrooms in Chicago.

Yes, I'd wear a tuxedo and watch all the high-society folks caper to my tunes. Someday I might even become part of a renowned symphony orchestra.

But a journalist? Preposterous! I wasn't even very keen on writing.

The teacher continued to gently nudge me in that direction, even wangling me a job as part-time cub reporter on the local newspaper. Soon I was hooked…I'd just navigated my first fork in the road of life.

Fate wasn't through with me, however. It appeared on the scene a half-dozen times during my service days in World War II. And it continued to poke and prod throughout my life…a missed airplane flight connection (it crashed)…a man I met for a casual breakfast (he hired me)…a wonderful woman I found purely by accident (she's my wife).

One of the strangest events happened because I hired a man who turned out to be totally unsuited for the job he was supposed to do. After considerable agonizing, I faced up to the decision and let him go. We parted company, more or less amiably.

He soon found a job he loved. After a year or two, he called and asked me to have lunch with the owner of the company he worked for.

Where Would This Lead?

That lunch led to a complete and major career change for *me*—one that brought me considerable joy for the rest of my business years. Go figure. The man I'd fired ended up doing *me* a favor!

Looking back, you can't help but ask, again and again, *what if?* And why? How about the road not taken? What if the coin had come up heads instead of tails?

Think about those grandchildren you adore. They're the product of a whole bunch of *what ifs.* What if you hadn't gone on that blind date? What if you'd married the person you already had your eye on, instead?

Later on, what if you hadn't suffered the bad break that forced you to start a new life in a new town? And what if your son or daughter hadn't met their future spouse on a crowded bus in that new town?

Fork after fork after fork, each choice changing your life in ways you could never foresee. And all of them add up to the joy of watching beloved grandchildren open presents on Christmas morning.

Big Actor Started Small

James Garner, the actor, tells of his early days in Los Angeles when he worked at a string of about 16 menial jobs and had no goal in life.

One day, he saw an acquaintance's car parked beside an office building. On sheer impulse, Garner turned in, found a parking spot and discovered his friend had become a talent agent.

An hour later, Garner had a non-speaking part in *The Caine Mutiny.*

"If there hadn't been an empty parking space, I would have returned to the filling station where I worked," he recalls. And, quite likely, never had a notable career in movies and television.

Then there's the story of a teenage boy, son of a family mired in Depression-era poverty on a farm in South Dakota. He was bright and ambitious, but his family was broke. There was no hope of raising the $300 needed to send him to the state university. He was trapped.

Then, he says, "Destiny showed a happier face. The face belonged to a man who drove a battered '34 Ford into our dusty driveway one August afternoon and asked for me."

The man was a recruiter for a business school in Minneapolis. It offered an 8-month course that cost just $150 and promised to prepare students for a career in business.

The boy sold his three 4-H calves to raise the money, promising his father that he'd return in time for spring planting. It was the critical beginning that led to a real college education and, eventually, a distinguished career in the United States Foreign Service.

Was it destiny? The hand of God? Just a lucky accident?

How *do* you account for the way that a letter lost in the mail opened the door to a satisfying career?

How *do* you explain why a broken toe brought good fortune? Or why an automobile accident ended up in a happy marriage for two 70-year-olds?

Those are just three of the many intriguing stories in this book that will set you thinking.

Grew Up During the Depression

Reminisce reader Ernest Webber put together his memories in a fine book called *Growing Up in the Ozarks.* Like so many of us, Ernest was a child of the Great Depression, raised in deep poverty.

One summer, he took a job selling vanilla extract and other food flavorings, trudging up and down steep dirt roads in the Ozarks. Some days he'd walk 20 miles and not reap a single order. The people he called on were as poor as he was.

It was miserable unrewarding work. But along the way, he met an attractive girl, and you know the rest. They wed, stayed in love through thick and thin and now have been married for over 50 years.

Ernest earned barely $50 that entire summer. Yet had he not taken the job, it's unlikely that he and Lavista ever would have met.

Was it only chance that brought them together?

That puzzlement is bound to loom large as you read the haunting-yet-happy stories in this book. And when you're finished, I feel sure you'll find yourself looking back over your own life to ponder your forks in the road: Was it fate, destiny, Divine Providence or plain dumb luck?

What a delicious mystery!

Chapter One

*W*hen Bad Breaks Become Blessings

Child's Disability Led Mom to Help Others

By Alice Marks, Colorado Springs, Colorado

WHEN our daughter Joyce was 18 months old, we learned she was profoundly deaf. I felt like I'd been kicked hard in the stomach.

Today, my husband and I aren't the same people who heard this shocking news so long ago. Between then and now, our family had much to learn—tolerance, patience, compassion and the ability to look beyond a handicap and see a precious happy toddler.

Slowly, acceptance came. "God doesn't send us problems like this and then abandon us," our priest said. A speech therapist told us, "Yes, you've got a problem, but it isn't the end of the world. You've got an intelligent child and a lot of work to do."

We began with the John Tracy correspondence course for deaf preschoolers. An early lesson was for me: "You are blessed among mothers, for you can lead such an interesting life." Much later I could agree, but there were many times I doubted it.

We concentrated on activities to sharpen Joyce's other senses. In one exercise, we drew stick men to represent action words and modeled whatever they were doing—running, walking, hopping, standing, sit-

LEAVING HOME. This photo was taken when Joyce Marks was 5 and bound for a school for the deaf. Mother Alice says, "So often handicapped children can pull a family apart. Ours was drawn together."

ting, falling. We were black and blue from falling, because that was Joyce's favorite.

Made Loud Discovery

After Joyce was fitted with a hearing aid to make her conscious of the little high-frequency hearing she had, she discovered she had a voice. Then she screamed all day. The high pitch was the only feedback she could get.

To help Joyce learn about the rhythms of speech, we put marches on the stereo, turned up the volume so she could feel the vibrations, and all seven of us marched, clapped and played follow the leader. We talked, counted, read and talked some more.

SIGN AND SMILE. Today, Joyce is a professional, a college grad and a mother. Thanks to her, Mom Alice enjoyed a career in special education.

When Joyce was 5, the dreaded day came when we took her to the State School for the Deaf in Council Bluffs, 200 miles away. The hardest part was being unable to explain that we weren't abandoning her. Looking back, I wonder how I could let her go.

Then a miracle happened. My husband was offered a job in Bloomington-Normal, Illinois, and the lab school at Illinois State University would accept Joyce in the deaf classes. She could live at home!

I began studying for a degree in deaf education, but one semester taught me I couldn't work with the deaf all day, then come home to a deaf child. I switched to speech pathology, working with all kinds of handicapped children. When I graduated, I worked as a speech therapist for the public schools.

More Good Signs

Meanwhile, Joyce continued to grow and learn. When signing was introduced, she and her classmates took to it immediately.

During high school, Joyce asked to attend the Illinois

School for the Deaf in Jacksonville. She studied hard, played on the volleyball team and enjoyed her time there. She graduated with a scholarship to the National Technical Institute for the Deaf in St. Paul, Minnesota.

Today, Joyce has been happily married for 16 years—she and her husband, also deaf, signed their vows in a beautiful ceremony—and has two darling little girls.

She's a well-adjusted homemaker, independent and artistic, and her sense of humor and caring ways are a joy to all of us.

Since my husband and I retired to Colorado, I've had time to reflect on all that happened. I estimate at least 1,000 children benefited from the therapy I provided—because Joyce's deafness led me to special education. What seemed like a tragedy produced many blessings.

Friend's Act of Mercy Revealed Hidden Talent

By Marjorie Baker, Bandera, Texas

ONE DAY I visited my longtime friend, florist Lillian McDowell, and found her in tears. She'd been diagnosed with cancer and needed surgery. What would happen to her business? It was her only means of support, and she had no family to help.

"I'm here for you," I said. "Teach me what to do." I couldn't believe my ears! I grew up believing I had no creative ability and had for years taken my flowers to Lillian to arrange.

Lillian studied me carefully,

NEW-FOUND TALENT. Marjorie Baker posed for this picture before a formal banquet in which she helped decorate the hall.

LOVELY LILLIAN looks ready to attend the formal, too. Photo was taken at the beginning of her battle with cancer.

without speaking. When she realized I was serious, she took my hands, smiling through her tears.

"Okay," she said. "Let's start with the basics."

By the time Lillian had her surgery, she'd taught me enough to keep the business afloat. When she came home from the hospital, she continued to teach me from her bed.

Soon I was doing it all. I had to recruit friends to help during busy periods and sometimes worked through the night to prepare for a wedding or funeral.

Even as Lillian weakened, she continued to be my teacher, critic and friend. Her faith in me, and her patient and thorough training, gave me the courage to accept this challenge. God gave me the strength to endure the long difficult days.

My greatest reward was knowing that, when Lillian lost her battle with cancer, there were no unpaid bills and there was money in the bank.

Lillian taught me not only how to run a flower shop, but to believe in myself and to use my imagination to create a variety of crafts.

My creations helped pay my son's college tuition and enabled me to give part of myself to others. Passing this gift on to my daughter and others has been a further blessing.

Lillian's battle with cancer was indeed a "bad break", but it was a blessing to fight alongside her. A simple act of kindness changed my life forever, showing once again that in giving, we receive.

FIRST JOB. Alice Schumacher sat for her teacher application photo in 1930. She taught her first class at the schoolhouse above, in Outlook, Montana, in September of that year.

Lost Mail Sent Teacher 2,000 Miles to New Home

By Alice Schumacher, Great Falls, Montana

IN 1930, at age 21, I received a bachelor's degree and teaching certificate from the University of Oregon. I mailed dozens of applications and photos, but no job offers came. Each day my hopes shrank, along with my savings.

At the end of August, I received a phone call. "This is the clerk of the school board in Roseburg, Oregon," the voice announced.

My surge of joy collapsed as the voice went on, "We sent you a contract, but as you did not sign and return it to us within the prescribed 30 days, it has been rescinded and the position filled."

"But I never received your contract!" I protested. "I'd be happy to accept!"

"It's too late, I'm afraid. As I said, the position has been filled. Sorry."

Stunned, I hung up. That job was the best I could have imagined. The salary was above average, and Roseburg was a progressive beautiful town only 75 miles from home. How could a letter possibly get lost traveling only 75 miles?

It was the end of summer and much too late to hope for an opening…I'd missed my best chance.

Then out of the blue I received a telegram offering me a job in northeast Montana. It was over 2,000 miles from home, almost in Canada, and the pay was minimal. The opening of school was only a week away. I wired my acceptance.

It took the balance of my savings to buy a cheap suitcase, footlocker, clothing suitable for Montana and a one-way train ticket to prairie oblivion.

The job kept me too busy for self-pity. The people in Montana were wonderful, and there were horses to ride. Two years later, I moved to a school 21 miles away.

By this time I had come to love Montana…and a young farmer. We married a year later and eventually enjoyed 50 devoted years together. We celebrated our golden anniversary with our five children and their families.

A teaching contract entrusted to the U.S. Postal Service must have been plucked from the system 68 years ago by some grinning gremlin who had a better ending in mind for my job search.

Ironically, after my husband and I tied the knot, he was appointed to a new job…as a postmaster.

BANG-UP MEETING made John and Thelma Ramsey's wedding day possible.

Fender Bender Answered Lonely Retiree's Prayer

By Thelma Ramsey, Tulsa, Oklahoma

AFTER retiring, I had many friends and stayed busy with church work. But deep down I was lonely and prayed for a nice man to come into my life. I never dreamed that prayer would be answered with a fender bender!

March 11, 1990 was cold, rainy and dreary, and I was running behind schedule on my way to church. As I drove through an intersection, *wham!* Another car—the same color, make and model as mine—struck my left fender. The driver had skidded while trying to stop.

No one was hurt and there wasn't much damage, so we exchanged information, and the man promised to call me. Then we went our separate ways to church.

John did call, and in that conversation and others that followed, we learned about each other. He was retired, too, and widowed. (I'd never married.) It was almost uncanny how much we had in common. We even have the same rare blood type.

We were married in a small beautiful ceremony on April 19, 1991. The years since have been the best and most fulfilling of my life.

It's scary to think that if I'd been on schedule that Sunday morning, we wouldn't have even met. He had his schedule, too, and was on time that day. The matter of a few seconds can and does change lives!

Stay in Orphanage Taught Independence, Self-Worth

By Henrietta Finch
Conway, Oregon

AFTER my mom died in 1942, Dad had it rough. He worked in a box factory in Arkansas and didn't make enough money to care for six children. We ate oatmeal for breakfast, pork and beans for lunch, and were lucky to get any supper.

Dad finally decided to put us

ORPHAN NO MORE. Henrietta Finch was all smiles on her 1957 wedding day with Nolan.

in the Baptist orphanage in Monticello, Arkansas. My four brothers were excited about having lots of other children to play with, but I was heartbroken.

The trip to the orphanage seemed like the longest of my life. But the superintendent was very kind and gracious, and I gradually got used to it—especially the three good meals a day. I actually liked the orphanage better than my brothers did, although I still missed Dad a lot.

After graduating from high school and finishing my first year of college, I met a wonderful man. During my senior year, Nolan and I were married in the church where we'd met.

Looking back, I probably wouldn't have attended college or met Nolan if I hadn't gone to the orphanage. I learned to be independent, gained some self-esteem and realized I could do almost anything if I set my mind to it. I am thankful to God for working things out in my life. He always knows best.

Strike Enabled Welder to Forge Thriving Business

By Glenn Taylor, Atlanta, Georgia

SHORTLY after World War II ended, I was laid off from a job at General Motors. So, I started a backyard welding shop with one portable welding machine and a pickup truck.

I was struggling to make a living when General Motors reopened, and I was recalled to my old job. After 3 days, the workers went out on strike.

When my few welding customers found out I'd gone back to GM, they began to look elsewhere. But by the time the strike ended about 3 months later, I was so busy I never even went back to pick up my 3 days' pay.

Today, my company employs over 400 people, and last year's sales exceeded $50 million. If GM hadn't had a strike, I probably would've continued working there until retirement.

Bad Break Was a Step in Right Direction

By Jo-Ann Brandt Engst, East Peoria, Illinois

IT'S STILL difficult to believe, but something as trivial as a broken toe changed my life in a positive way.

When my husband and I retired, I started a daily physical fitness program to stay active. After 4 months, I was in a workout routine that had me feeling good.

Then it happened...I was walking across the room and somehow managed to wrap my toe around a chair leg. The result was a broken toe —no big deal. But 6 to 8 weeks of inactivity didn't look very appealing.

While doing some reading, I found a magazine article that de-

PRETTY PICTURES are a snap for Jo-Ann, who used a timer to take her own photo above. On facing page are: crimson maple in Maryland; snowy egret on a fishing boat in Mt. Dora, Florida; "Cowtown" wagons in Wichita, Kansas; and award-winning Florida sunset scene.

scribed a photo contest. The contest was open to pros and amateurs alike. I was no pro, but figured I had nothing to lose. I decided to enter some of the photos from my albums.

I sent off a package of scenics and promptly forgot about it. Imagine my surprise to be called a few weeks later to hear that one of my photos (bottom right) was a winner.

Since then, I've taken many more photos for publication. The toe has healed, and I ended up with a fulfilling hobby that blossomed into a new career opportunity.

One Brother's Misfortune Opened Door to Another's Joy

By Sharlotte Rau, Grand Rapids, Michigan

MY UNCLE JELTE and his large family lived on a dairy farm near the Canadian border in Sumas, Washington. In the late 1940s, an old spinal injury from a slip on ice began to worsen. Soon he could no longer put on his own socks.

His only hope was surgery at the Mayo Clinic in Minnesota, followed by months of lying flat on his back with nursing care.

The only nurse the family knew was Olive DeJong, a cousin of Uncle Jelte's wife. Olive was an "old maid city lady" living with her mother in Michigan.

Uncle Jelte didn't even know her, but to

CHANGED THEIR NAMES. Olive DeJong and Ralph Visser were married November 25, 1948—the day the retired bachelor and old maid nurse gave up those monikers for good.

save costs, went to her home to recuperate from the operation in April 1948. His brother Ralph, a semi-retired bachelor, flew out to help him get settled, then returned to Washington.

During Uncle Jelte's recovery, a budding romance began between Ralph and Olive via the mail. When Uncle Jelte came home that fall, Olive came along for a 2-week visit. She returned to Michigan with a diamond ring.

On Thanksgiving Day 1948, the retired bachelor and old maid nurse were married. They assumed they were too old to have children, so they settled into Ralph's small house. But God had some surprises in store.

Just after their first anniversary, a baby was born—an answer to fervent prayer. Within a year, another was on the way.

Suddenly, retirement was out of the question. Ralph needed a full-time job! He and Olive bought a farm and moved in just before their second child was born. It would be another 18 years before Ralph retired again.

I was the first miracle baby, and my brother, Andrew, was the second.

If it hadn't been for a slip on the ice by Uncle Jelte, my parents wouldn't have met, and my brother and I wouldn't exist. We don't always understand, but God's way is best!

By the way, Uncle Jelte remained mobile well into his 90s. The surgery turned out to be a blessing for him, too.

If Ship Had Been Shipshape, They Never Would Have Met

By Dorothy Wurdeman, Lynn, Massachusetts

IN 1946, I was an Army nurse on a hospital ship headed to Okinawa. When the ship broke down, we stopped in Panama for repairs. That's where I met Edgar, an Army corporal from Nebraska.

A GOLDEN TOAST. Edgar and Dorothy celebrated their 50th anniversary in 1996.

I was an officer, and it was against orders to fraternize with enlisted men, but Edgar and I did meet at the PX. We hit it off and planned to meet again, but we didn't realize how soon that would be.

When the ship was repaired, we set out for Okinawa—but it broke down again. Back to Panama! The ship never did get to Okinawa. It was ordered back to California, and I began working at a hospital in Van Nuys.

Edgar came to California, too, to attend college in Los Angeles. When I returned home to Massachusetts, we stayed in touch by phone. He proposed during one of those calls, and we were married in my hometown September 9, 1946.

The "bad break" of those hospital ship breakdowns turned into a lifelong blessing.

Stalled Chevy Reunited High School Companions

By Norma Poole
Auburndale, Florida

BUCK AND I grew up in Tignall, Georgia and dated occasionally through high school. He finished school 2 years before I did, left for college, then moved to Florida.

I went to nurse's training at Emory University. In the next 10 years, we rarely saw each other, though we dated if we happened to be back in town at the same time.

ARMY NURSE Norma posed for this photo in World War II. She didn't know then she'd reunite with a special high school friend.

World War II came along, and we each served 4 years—Buck in the Army, I in the Army Nurse Corps. After my discharge, I planned to go back to Emory, but was talked into taking a job as a public health nurse in my home county.

One morning on the way to work, my car stalled in Tig-

CAR-TROUBLE COUPLE. Wed for nearly 50 years, Buck and Norma Poole owe it all to a broken-down Chevy.

nall, 10 miles from my office. Buck was coming across the street and saw me—I didn't even know he was in town—and helped me get to the filling station.

The mechanic gave the car a "temporary fix" and told me to come back that afternoon so he could finish the job. When I returned, Buck was waiting there. We were married 6 months later.

I've always kidded Buck, "If my old Chevrolet hadn't conked out on me, I wouldn't have gotten into trouble." My Ford-salesman husband's reply: "You should've been driving a Ford."

Pilot's Clipped Wings Led To Reunion...and a Safe Life

By Mary Anderson, Jamestown, Kansas

WHEN my husband-to-be enrolled in the Army ROTC in 1954, he was asked if he'd ever had hay fever. He hadn't, but for some reason when he filled out the form, he said yes. The answer went unnoticed as John proceeded through training.

After graduation and officers' training, he was sent to helicopter school. John was thrilled. He loved flying, and we appreciated the extra flight pay.

Then someone noticed the hay fever response on John's ROTC questionnaire, so he was washed out of helicopter school. John was devastated.

His next assignment was in Germany—another blow. We'd be separated for 2-1/2 months before I could join him.

As it turned out, living in Germany was like an 18-month

FAMILY REUNION began in Germany in 1959, when serviceman John Anderson (right) arrived. John is greeted by Hein, Gesa and Greta Ficke, relatives of John's wife, Mary, who'd never met them. Strong friendships continue today—all because of John's bad break in helicopter school.

honeymoon. Best of all, we got acquainted with my father's brother and his family, whom I'd never met.

When our first child was born, my parents came for a cherished homecoming and family reunion. My cousin Gesa later moved to the United States.

John's helicopter school classmates ended up serving extended tours of duty and flying missions in Vietnam. By then we were safely home in Kansas, farming.

Back-to-Back Accidents Brought Couple Together

By Pegeen Bull, Freeport, Florida

MY DAUGHTER Bonnie kept telling me about a man she wanted me to meet, a butcher in the Pennsylvania store where she worked.

It was 1989, and I'd been widowed for a while. But my husband and I had been together for 26 years, and I still wasn't too sure about this dating game.

A few weeks later, Bonnie's foot and ankle were crushed when her horse spooked during a trail ride. Bonnie was 5 months pregnant. The baby was fine, but Bonnie's leg needed surgery.

After a month, her leg in a cast and hobbling on crutches, Bonnie decided to go shopping with me so she could visit her coworkers. A tall broad-shouldered butcher with thick silky hair asked her, "When are you going to freshen, heifer?" I was a lifelong farmer, so that question made an impression on me.

Later, I asked Bonnie about him. It was Frank—the butcher she'd been trying to get me to meet!

I kept thinking about him and finally got a friend to ask Frank if he'd go out with me. We had dinner, took a walk, then sat at a picnic table and talked for hours. I was *very* impressed.

Two days later, I broke my back and was hospitalized 60 miles from home. On the second day, Frank arrived with flowers. He came back every day until I was released.

When I came home, I was in a wheelchair, and Bonnie still had a cast on her leg. Neither of us could do any work on the farm. Frank arranged his schedule so he could do most of the chores.

On Labor Day, Frank asked my family how they'd feel "if I married your mother". He hadn't even asked me yet. They gave their happy approval.

We got married in October and rode the mile from church to the farm on a hay wagon. Over 40 cars followed, blowing their horns and scaring everyone's cattle along the way. Our reception was in the barn, and the fire department put up a tent for eating and visiting.

Both Bonnie's accident and mine were certainly bad breaks...but she gained a new stepfather and I, a wonderful husband. Frank and I have been married 9 years, and now we take care of each other.

HAY RIDE. Frank and Pegeen Bull rode home from their wedding in style in 1989.

Hand Injury Provided Just The Break This GI Needed

By John Parente, West Lafayette, Indiana

IN 1952, while working to earn money for college, I was drafted into the Army. I'd completed 3 years of music study at Indiana University. Now my senior year was being taken away!

Months later, while stationed in Germany, I was playing catch with our master sergeant, an excellent athlete. He hurled a brand-new softball at me with incredible speed, and I grabbed it with my bare hand.

When I started to throw the ball back, I noticed my little finger was dangling. Pain began shooting up my wrist. My hand was fractured in three places.

The next day, I looked at the cast on my hand. I thought of my college studies, the years of playing clarinet and saxophone, the lessons, the dance jobs, the parades, the football games. I stormed to the colonel's office and demanded to see him.

WHAT A BREAK! Fractured hand earned John Parente the duty he preferred.

Through misty eyes, I explained that I couldn't spend the next 16 months without music. To my surprise, the colonel agreed with me completely. Within a week, I was transferred to the 1st Division Band in Kitzingen, Germany.

That year could not have been more pleasurable or beneficial. I became the band's solo clarinetist and spent the next 16 months playing concerts and parades. I got valuable playing experience, met excellent musicians and made great friends.

What a break that broken hand turned out to be!

Military Played Cupid For Three Generations In Her Family

By Betty Hussey, Old Bridge, New Jersey

IF IT weren't for a couple of wars, my life wouldn't be as it is. The military played a big role in my family.

In 1918, a young man named Gus Howes was stationed with the cavalry in Hawaii. A buddy told Gus about his sister Rita back in Brooklyn. After the war, Gus and Rita got together. That resulted in marriage—and me.

MATCHED BY MILITARY. In 1918, Betty Hussey's dad, Gus Howes (top, left), heard about his future wife. WAVE Betty (center, 1945) met her mate in the Navy. And Navy daughter Patricia married a Marine, 1991.

During World War II, I was a "corpsman" in the Navy WAVES and had a wonderful Marine for a patient. That resulted in marriage, too, and nine children.

Two of our children later joined the Navy, and one met a wonderful Marine and married him.

There are 10 grandchildren so far…let's hope *they* don't have to worry about any wars.

Secret Admirer Rescued Damsel in Distress

By Ann Coutcher
Crest Hill, Illinois

WHEN I was hired as a police officer, I had to take 10 weeks' training 7 hours from home. Leaving my fiance behind was difficult, but I knew this path would greatly improve my life. Little did I know!

I didn't know it, but another trainee at camp had noticed me and told his friends he'd seen the woman he was going to marry. David hadn't even spoken to me, and I didn't acknowledge him in the least—after all, I had a fiance, and my future was pretty well mapped. Still, he was searching for the right opportunity to meet me.

A REAL KNOCKOUT. That's what David Coutcher encountered—in more ways than one. He and Ann were married in 1992, a blessing from a bad break.

One morning we took our physical training in stifling heat. David was playing basketball, and I was running on the track. When he went up for a shot, he glanced up and saw me slumped on the track, passed out. He ran over immediately and administered CPR. I recovered just fine, and we married 3 years later.

Today, he says he wasn't there the first time I fell, but he'll always be there to catch me from now on.

Chance Meeting on Train
Put Love on Track

By Mary Mumgaard, Lincoln, Nebraska

A FAVORITE COUSIN went down with his plane in the aftermath of World War II. My younger sister and I took a 10-hour train ride to Chicago for the funeral. The sad days moved slowly, but one night we finally boarded another train for home.

The hours dragged as the train seemed to stop at every town. Darkness turned to dawn. Passengers began moving

WHAT A GROUP! This happy gathering at Christmas, 1990, wouldn't have been possible if Milo and Mary Mumgaard (upper left corner) hadn't bumped into one another on a train in the 1940s. Thirty-seven of their progeny posed in this picture. That number has now risen to 45!

toward the dining car. A few seats away, I saw a handsome Air Force lieutenant lowering his bag from the overhead rack.

He replaced his bag and turned in our direction to ask us to breakfast. But a priest happening down the aisle greeted him and suggested the lieutenant join him. Disappointed, my sister and I went back to watching the view.

A short time later, we heard a voice from the aisle: "Good morning. Going far?" The lieutenant was back—and he's stayed for 50 years.

Had I not made that sad train trip to Chicago for a funeral, I might never have met the most important person in my life, or had my 10 wonderful children, 19 grandchildren and 2 great-grandchildren.

Housewife Transformed Herself Into Accomplished Professional

By Katherine Smith, Corvallis, Oregon

MY LIFE changed forever—the day someone else got appendicitis.

I was typical 1960s housewife, obsessed with keeping a clean house, cook-

CAN DO. If Katherine Smith could raise seven kids, she could tackle any job! That's Katherine at top, and alongside husband Rollie with their children.

ing nutritious meals and raising good kids. I made endless batches of cookies for the Cub Scouts and PTA, taught Sunday school and helped with Camp Fire Girls. My house was the center of the neighborhood.

It was a good life, but after our seventh child was born, it became clear my husband needed a second job, or I had to contribute to our income.

I hadn't worked for over 16 years, but I had secretarial skills. I read the "help wanted" ads every day. Finally one caught my eye: "Part-time secretarial. Must have excellent typing skills and a pleasant outgoing personality."

That fit me, except for the personality. I'd always considered myself a loner. In school I was the last one chosen for the team, the wallflower at the dance. This job wasn't for me. But I looked at the ad every day for a week.

The next Monday, the ad was gone. Now it would be safe to call. The job had to be filled, but at least I'd have been brave enough to inquire.

I called. The job wasn't filled. Could I come in for an interview?

I interviewed with three people in the County Health Department's Mental Health Division. An hour after I got home, the phone rang. I was offered the job!

Ready to Work

I excitedly called my best friend and my husband and told the children as they came home from school. I planned my first week's wardrobe and counted the change in the piggy bank for a haircut. I'd start on Wednesday, after a routine interview with the county health officer.

That interview seemed to go well, but shortly after I got home, the secretary called. The health officer wouldn't approve hiring me. Because I had seven children, he didn't think I'd be dependable.

Not dependable? I was the most dependable person I knew! The Midwestern work ethic was in my bones!

Had I ever missed a Sunday school class, a PTA meeting or teacher's conference? Didn't I make sure the boys had good basketball shoes, that Cindy had a Pep Club outfit and figure out how to make payments on Kim's viola? Wasn't dinner on the table every night at 6, whether I felt good or not?

I had a good cry. Then I went back to the ads.

The next morning, the phone rang. The "other woman" who'd been hired had appendicitis. Would I help them out and take the job?

Well, I worked at the Mental Health Division for 17 years, and it truly changed my life. I gained respect for myself and my abilities, and the staff was glad that I could do six things at once.

When our children were grown, I earned my bachelor's degree by attending college nights and weekends. Then I decided to go for my dream. I quit my job, went to graduate school and earned a master's in social work.

My first professional evaluation included this: "An excellent therapist, very dependable, a most pleasant outgoing personality."

And all because "the other woman" got appendicitis.

A "BIRD OF PARADISE" it wasn't, but it did unite Melvin and Hazel Miller.

Series of Bad Breaks Couldn't Stop This Marriage

By Hazel Miller
Terre Haute, Indiana

I WAS a single mother of two daughters, not interested in another marriage. But when my youngest begged me to take her to a picnic sponsored by a single parents' organization, I relented.

During the picnic, a bird flew over us and left a calling card right on my head! I was so embarrassed.

A kind man named Melvin Miller took out a handkerchief and wiped the mess from my head. Then he asked if he could come by that night and take me for a motorcycle ride.

Evening came, and he didn't, so I got into my night-clothes to watch television. Then a rap came at the door—I wasn't stood up after all!

Melvin's backpack had blown off his cycle on the way over, scattering the contents along the road,

HAPPY AS EVER. Hazel and Melvin posed for this photo on their 19th anniversary.

and he'd had to go back to retrieve them.

Melvin and I dated for 6 years, until 1976. Realizing we were very much in love, we decided to put our faith in God and get married.

On our wedding day, Melvin arrived late, looking pale and nervous. After the ceremony, he rushed me through the gift opening almost to the point of rudeness. He wasn't his normal self.

When the reception ended, I found out why. "Honey, you're going to have to take me to the hospital," Melvin said. "I'm having a kidney stone attack."

I rushed him to the emergency room, still wearing my long pink dress and carnation corsage. When the doctor learned we'd just gotten married, he gave us a serious look. "It's too bad we don't make double beds for occasions like this," he said.

Melvin was admitted, and I left the hospital in the wee hours, thankful no one else was in sight. Our car was plastered with "Just Married" signs and smelled of Limburger cheese (some wise guy had put it near the engine).

But I was too upset to notice. The bride was behind the wheel, minus the groom.

After I got home, I decided to drive to my sister's house. That was a big mistake. I backed the car into a fence and killed the motor. Then the car wouldn't start.

So I did what any sensible bride would do. I went inside, sat down on the couch and cried.

The next morning, a neighbor helped me untangle my car from the fence, and it started right up. I was soon holding hands with my husband, who spent the next 3 days in the hospital.

When our pastor heard our tale of woe, he laughed and said, "Anyone having such a bad start is bound to have a good marriage." More than 20 years later, we know he was right.

Insensitive Remark Motivated Retiree to Computer Wizardry

By Freddie Steese, Lancaster, California

HARD-DRIVIN'. Freddie Steese loves tinkering with technology.

BORN IN 1915, I've never had a dull moment in my life. A high school mechanical drawing teacher got me enthusiastic about engineering, and that became my life's work.

After retiring, I had open-heart surgery. That was when my life really started to change. During my rehabilitation, I took a college course in drawing and painting. My professor suggested I take a course in color and design, too. I'd known the instructor of that course for years, so I asked him about it.

"It's all computers," he replied. "You're too old." That did it. Nobody tells me I'm too old.

"I was into computers (Teletype machines) when you were wearing diapers," I told him. I can't remember anything ever making me so irate.

I picked up a few older computers at a secondhand store, then headed for the library. Refurbishing and upgrading computers turned into a rewarding pastime and a lucrative business. Helping others with their computer problems has become an important part of my life—along with oil painting.

The teacher who made the remark about my age really turned my life around for the better.

Wartime Marriage Led British Family to America

By Pamela Williams, Towanda, Pennsylvania

I WAS 5 years old when World War II began in Europe back in 1939. One of my earliest memories is of a man coming to our home about 25 miles outside London to fit us for gas masks. Over the next 6 years, we never left home without them.

My father was in the Royal Air Force. He dug an air-raid shelter in our garden, and we used it a lot at first. But during the blitz, the air raids happened night and day, so life simply went on.

Once there was a "dog fight" right above our house —and I mean at tree-top level—between a Spitfire and a Messerschmidt.

We were having supper then, and Mother told us to go under the stairs. Instead, I opened the back door to watch. The German plane dropped a load of bombs quite close that night,

FRIENDLY GI'S posed with Pamela Williams (left), her mother and her aunt Phyllis in 1944.

breaking windows and cracking a wall in our house.

But we were lucky because we lived in the country. Our town was a "reception area", where people from bombed-out London came to live. Everyone took in evacuees without a thought of being paid. Paid with what? These people had lost everything. The evacuees came without ration books, but we shared what little we had. For 2 years, I slept in an armchair.

Once we took in two little girls, and my grandmother next door took in their two brothers. They'd been living in the London underground and looked like urchins. They had nothing but the dirty clothes they were wearing—and fleas.

Carried Milk for Miles

My mother cleaned and cooked for seven to nine people in our very small house. The only food that wasn't rationed was the vegetables in our garden. Every night for years, I walked 2 miles to a farm with a 2-quart pail for extra milk. We had a fireplace in every room, but lit one only when someone was ill. We bathed once a week, using water heated on the cook stove.

Then the Yanks came. There were two U.S. Air Force bases nearby, and with an older sister at home, our house soon was full of GI's.

They talked about their hometowns and families, trying to enjoy a little home life. They knew we had nothing, so they always brought something—fruit, macaroni and cheese, canned meat, dried eggs, ham and candy bars. I hadn't tasted candy in years.

When the war ended, there were really no winners. The austerity and rationing continued. There were jobs and meager paychecks for the men who came home to rebuild England, but nothing much to buy. Many families began leaving for Canada and Australia with the government's blessing.

My sister married an American serviceman in 1944 and emigrated to the United States to join him in 1946. Her war-bride marriage changed the course of my life.

By 1947, my sister had persuaded my parents to start proceedings to emigrate to the States. The most important requirement was that we be responsible for ourselves.

WAR BRIDE'S WEDDING DAY. The whole family posed before Pamela Williams' girlhood home. Note bomb shelter entrance at far left! Pamela's sister and her GI husband are third and fourth from left, first row. Pamela's in front, wearing white dress.

We'd be ineligible for welfare—if we didn't make it by working, we'd be sent back to England.

After 2 years, the American Embassy finally approved our request. My just-married brother took most of our furniture. Mom had to sell many of her treasures, including her engagement ring, to pay for our passage.

Sailed in Steerage

My parents and I departed with one steamer trunk and a suitcase holding everything we had, including my one doll and the only ball I'd ever owned. Our tourist-class cabin was as deep in the ship as you could go.

The morning of May 26, we rose early to salute the Statue of Liberty. Oh, what a sight! When the ship docked, my sister and brother-in-law were waiting for us in a new 1949 Ford for a glorious ride to Ithaca, New York. It was dark when we arrived, and all the twinkling lights of the city seemed to welcome us.

My sister worked at a soda fountain and asked the next morning if I wanted to go along. I didn't know a nickel from a dime, had never eaten an ice cream sundae and hadn't heard of tuna fish salad. But I learned quickly and worked there most of the summer.

Whole Family Worked Hard

I later found a cashier's job at a grocery store, working after school and on Saturdays. Mom and Dad found jobs, our apartment had indoor plumbing—even a bathroom—and Dad bought a car. We were really living the good life.

When I graduated in 1952, I'd saved $500, which was a lot of money in those days. I spent it on my wedding a week later.

Five years to the day after my arrival in America, I became a citizen, and I've never regretted it for a minute.

Because of World War II, I never really had a childhood. Mother and Father had little time for me as they scratched out a life for us in a war-torn country.

Today, we hear a lot about deprived childhoods and kids going wrong because of it. That's tommyrot. I know, because no one was more deprived than we were during the war.

I often wonder what turn

COMMENDATIONS. Pam Williams' family was commended by Queen Elizabeth and King George for helping British citizens in need during wartime.

my life would have taken without the war, the rationing, the devastation. World War II changed my life forever. I thank my lucky stars I was able to immigrate here. I know that I live in the best country in the world.

Chapter Two

The Advice I've Valued Most

Father's Patient Example
Made Her a Better Parent

By DeLila Chrisp, Worland, Wyoming

FROM THE TIME my legs were long enough to reach the clutch on our old Farmall tractor, I worked summers in the hayfield for my dad. The new kid always started out on the dump rake, picking up the hay the sweep left behind.

My second summer out, in the mid-1960s, Dad bought a brand-new red-and-yellow dump rake. When he brought it

BIG JOB, LITTLE GIRL. DeLila Chrisp expertly handles this Farmall H in 1972. She's pulling a hayrake she helped break in a few years before.

home, we all ran out to "ooh and aah" over it. It was the first new piece of haying equipment we'd ever had. I felt so privileged to use it.

One hot July day, we'd finished stacking on one meadow and were ready to move to the next. To get to the second meadow, we had to go around a grove of cottonwoods or go through a small opening about halfway down the grove.

I knew the new rake would fit through this opening—I'd seen Dad pull it through. Without giving it a second thought, I headed for that narrow opening.

I tried my hardest to get that rake through, but I didn't have Dad's experience. The right wheel wrapped itself around a big old cottonwood tree. At that moment, I didn't want to face another minute of life—let alone my father.

Dad had always been very understanding and patient with his children, but we'd never done something this bad. My strongest emotion wasn't fear, though. It was profound sadness at what I'd done to the new rake that Dad had saved and sacrificed so hard to buy.

She Faced the Music

Dad and my brother, Dave, were in the next meadow and didn't have a clue what had happened. I climbed off the tractor on wobbly legs and walked over. Dad stopped the tractor and pushed down the throttle so he could hear me.

"You got troubles?" he asked.

I spilled out the whole story. I'll never forget Dad's words as he climbed down from the tractor. "Well, those things can happen to anybody," he said. "Let's go see what we can do about it."

Now I'm a parent myself, and whenever I'm about to lose it with my teenagers, I remember that incident. Though I'll never be as patient as Dad was that day, his example surely has saved my children much grief. I'm convinced it molded my attitude for life. From all of us: Thanks, Dad!

PATIENT POP, Paul Smith, as he appears today. Paul smiles down from the same tractor seat he occupied on the day his daughter describes in this story.

Oh, Fudge!
Candy-Making
Mishap No Cause
For Tears

By Anna-Margaret O'Sullivan
Franklin, Indiana

WHEN I WAS 10, in the late 1920s, my mother taught me how to make fudge. In those days, fudge making was the first kitchen skill a little girl acquired.

SWEET MEMORIES of making fudge and Mother's advice are recalled by author (above) as an adult.

Mom had only shown me how to do it once, but when she went upstairs with a headache one afternoon, I eagerly asked if I could make some fudge. When I repeated the recipe correctly, she gave her permission.

I measured my sugar, cocoa, milk and butter and set the kettle over a burner on our old-time coal oil stove. I stirred and stirred until my arm ached.

Knowing when the candy was done was the tricky part. It seemed to be done, but it wasn't crystallizing properly. With serious misgivings, I buttered a large Pyrex pie plate and poured the fudge into it.

Needed Mom's Help

The fudge remained glossy and sticky, and I longed for Mother's input, but I didn't want to disturb her.

Then I remembered a step I'd seen Mother use. I poured cold water into a dishpan and carefully lowered the pie plate filled with molten fudge into it. Crack!

Pyrex or not, that molten fudge and cold water was too much for that pie plate—a long-ago wedding gift. I had to tell Mother what happened. I climbed the stairs as if I were going to the guillotine.

When Mother understood why I was sobbing and stammering, she sat up and took me in her arms. "Don't cry, honey," she said soothingly. "It was only a plate. It's too bad it broke, but no dish is worth tears. You didn't break it on purpose. It was an accident." Then she went downstairs with me to supervise another batch of fudge.

Mother's compassion reduced my near-tragedy to the status of an unfortunate accident. I absorbed this lesson and used it for the benefit of my own children years later: Nothing broken by accident is worth tears, and no one is punished or scolded for accidents.

Papa's Simple Advice Still Resonates Years Later

By Faye Field, Longview, Texas

WHEN I was a schoolgirl back in the late 1920s, I took a long hard history test and made the highest grade in our class. I could scarcely wait to tell my father! I felt sure he'd be proud of me—enough, perhaps, to give me a dime instead of a nickel to spend on candy at the store.

I hurried home down 2 miles of railroad tracks, then rushed to Papa, who was reading by the fireside. "Papa, look at my history test!" I exclaimed. "I made 100. I'm the only one in the class who got every answer right."

I waited, standing first on one foot, then the other. I even extended my hand for the anticipated coin. But Papa continued to look at my paper.

At last he said, "Just remember that what you don't know will fill volumes."

I was crestfallen. But as time has passed, I've come to realize that my father's simple

GOOD STUDENT Faye Field posed for this photo on the family farm in the 1920s.

statement was one of the most profound pieces of advice I've ever received.

Whenever I get puffed up by some bit of knowledge that my coworkers might not have learned yet, I think of Papa's advice and am humbled.

Mom Helped Expectant Daughter Sift Through Excessive Advice

By Theresa Holmes, Arvada, Colorado

THE ADVICE I value most came from my mother. When I was pregnant with my first child, she said I'd get more advice than I could possibly use, and that if I tried to follow all of it, I'd go nuts.

Mom told me to listen to everyone's advice, then use the good sense God gave me and do whatever I thought was best. She also told me never to tell anyone I wouldn't follow their suggestions, just to thank them kindly for their concern.

Thanks, Mom...it worked!

Neighbor's Helping Hand Gave Her a Green Thumb

By Beth Hayward
Boulder, Colorado

A GARDENING GURU. Warren Hering was generous with advice.

WHEN I was a young bride during the 1950s, my husband and I moved to a small college town. Our next-door neighbor, Warren Hering, had a backyard that was filled with colorful flowers, and he generously shared the bounty of his vegetable garden with the whole neighborhood.

I was fascinated and awed by Warren's gardening expertise. How did he always have different flowers blooming every week from spring through the first frost? I'd grown up in the big city of Detroit and had never even grown a geranium.

I hung over the fence pestering him with questions: "Why

FRIENDSHIP BLOOMS. Beth Hayward (right) remains dear friends with Warren Hering's daughter, Louise, who lives nearby. "The vegetable photo was taken in my backyard in 1970," Beth says. "It proves Warren's tutoring was a success."

do you cut the poppies off now? Do the beans all ripen at the same time? What are those flowers called? Why do you put stakes around the tomatoes?"

Warren's yard made ours look like the city dump. Could I grow a garden? I decided to try, and Warren patiently tutored me all summer, thus changing my life.

Planting seeds, hoeing weeds, watching tomatoes swell and turn red—all this fed my hungry soul after a hard day's work putting my hubby through college. I fell in love with the feel of dirt between my fingers.

I never thanked Warren enough for those lessons. I realize now what a great gift I received. At 63, I'm still planting and hoeing and watching.

Not long ago, a young bachelor bought the house next door. He called over the fence, "My name's Kevin, and this is my first house. I sure like your garden. But I don't know what's growing in my yard. Can you tell me if this is a flower or a weed?"

I leaned over the fence, identified his weeds and named the flowers pushing up through the soil. Later, I told my husband, "I was being Warren Hering this morning."

Thank you, Warren. Now maybe I can pass on your wonderful gift.

Nurse's Insight Prompted A Wise Switch In Careers

By Julia Kapinos
Norwich, Connecticut

DURING World War II, I was a Red Cross volunteer at our local hospital on nights and weekends. After working in the business world all day, I found tremendous satisfaction in helping people at night. By and by, I was becoming interested in the hospital environment.

RED CROSS VOLUNTEER Julia Kapinos as she appeared in 1945. An important decision lay ahead.

One evening, I was working with a senior student nurse and realized that she was watching me. I asked if anything was wrong. She just turned away and went about her duties.

Just before my shift ended, I confronted Ms. Rodgers. Why was she constantly watching me? Instead of answering my question, she asked one of her own. "Miss Julia, what do you do for a living?"

I told her I was an assistant office manager for Sears Roebuck. "You're wasted there," she quickly responded. "Why not come into nursing? You appear to have the knack for it, and

RIGHT CHOICE! Nearly 50 years after accepting wise advice, Julia is all smiles.

you're very good with the patients." I was so flattered all I could say was, "Thank you, Ms. Rodgers."

As I drove home, I thought about our conversation. Even after a good night's sleep, it lingered with me. For the next few days I was in turmoil.

Should I continue working at Sears Roebuck or venture into the field of medicine? Mama was a nurse. So were my two sisters, a niece, a cousin and an aunt. Why shouldn't I?

Courses Would Be Tough

My biggest concern was the course work. I'd been out of school for 4 years. Could I compete with the new high school graduates who'd taken nursing preparation classes?

I eventually applied to the hospital where I volunteered and attended summer school to prepare for the medical courses. After passing an entrance exam, I was admitted to nursing school.

The 3 years that followed were exciting, memorable and rewarding. Graduation day seemed to come quickly, and I was starting a new career.

It will soon be 50 years since my graduation from nursing school, and I've never regretted it. I'm still nursing and love every minute. It's so gratifying to see someone recover from being desperately ill and then to hear them say, "Thank you."

If I could see Ms. Rodgers today, I'd give her a great big hug for introducing me to the noblest of professions.

Nanna's Sage Advice Helped Dreams Come True

By Cookie Curci-Wright
San Jose, California

WISDOM AND BEAUTY. When author took advice from Nanna Isolina, (above) it changed her life forever.

AS Christmas approached in 1985, I was in no mood for revelry. I'd just lost my job and had all but decided not to celebrate Christmas.

For over 25 years, I'd put my dreams of being a writer on hold while I worked as a secretary. It didn't offer much of a creative outlet, but it paid the bills—and now it was gone.

I'd also put off getting married, so here I was in my mid-40s, with no job, no writing career and no Mr. Right. Not one of my lifelong plans had materialized.

I was deep in the doldrums when my Nanna Isolina invited me to her home for a Christmas visit. Though I'd been meaning to visit her for some time, I tried to think of an excuse not to go. She was almost 90 now—what could we have to say to each other after all these years?

I wanted to keep the memory of how it used to be—our laughter filling the kitchen as we planned and daydreamed about my future. Now it was obvious none of my plans would come true, and I didn't want to see her disappointment. But I couldn't refuse her invitation.

What Would Visit Bring?

When I arrived at Nanna's on Christmas Eve, she appeared more fragile than I remembered, but her eyes still twinkled. "Come in, come in, *bella mia*," she said. Nanna had called me *bella mia* (my beautiful) since childhood.

She led me to her cozy kitchen and sat me in Grandpa's big empty armchair at the head of the table. Everywhere I looked, I saw happy family memories and treasured keepsakes—a wall full of baby pictures, a Christmas tree decorated with ornaments made by Nanna's grandchildren, her beloved Nativity scene.

Before I knew it, I began to feel like a kid again. My hopes and dreams were renewed, along with my faith in the

SUNDAY DINNER at Grandpa Sal and Nanna Isolina's house brought the whole family together in 1955. Author is second from left.

Christmas spirit. We sipped coffee and dunked cookies, chattering like girls. The years melted away. We talked for hours.

Nanna predicted that, in the new year, I would find satisfaction in a writing career, and that, with a little more patience and faith, I would find Mr. Right. I smiled, reminding her that I was a middle-aged woman now, not the impressionable girl who once sat on her knee.

Nanna tenderly scolded me for not having enough faith in myself, or in her predictions. "You're not listening," she said. "How can you become a good writer if you don't have faith and listen?"

I spent all that week with Nanna, listening and taking notes while she retold endless family stories. I filled page after page with her reminiscences, though I had no idea what

NANNA WAS RIGHT! Cookie Curci-Wright became a published writer in 1988, thanks to her grandmother's belief in her.

to do with them. But Nanna wanted me to write, so I did.

The next year, I submitted several of Nanna's memories to my community newspaper.

The articles were so well-received that I was offered my own weekly nostalgia column, which I still write. I also met Mr. Right—Dan *Wright*. We were married just before Christmas.

Nanna wasn't here to see her predictions come true. But somehow I know that on that last visit, she knew exactly what the future held for me.

Husband's Challenge Pushed Her to Follow Her Dreams

By Becky Borland, Thornville, Ohio

WHEN I started my career with the post office, I had a chance to go out on different details. I was rather nervous, wondering whether I could do these jobs well—and do a good job at home at the same time. I couldn't let my family down.

My husband's response was, "No guts, no glory." My goal was to be a postmaster, and to fulfill that dream I would have to prove I could handle the details I was assigned.

To make a long story short, I served a lot of details for the U.S. Postal Service. Today, I'm postmaster at the Buckeye Lake (Ohio) Post Office. Without my husband's challenge and his confidence in me, I don't know if that would've happened.

'The Two Mavises' Led Her To Career Moves, Husband

By Nicles Leary, Live Oak, Florida

I WAS WORKING in a small Scottish town as a midwife, doing home deliveries, when a former coworker named Mavis told me about a job in Canada that might interest me. I applied and spent 5 years in Kingston, Ontario as a nursing supervisor in obstetrics.

I'd been interested in Eskimos for some time, so next I worked in a small hospital at Frobisher Bay in the Northwest Territories, just south of the Arctic Circle. I spent 2 years looking after Eskimos and doing home visits—an experience I'll always cherish.

My next move was to Florida. I was working in a pediatrician's office when another woman named Mavis entered my life and changed it forever. She introduced me to my husband, Joe, with whom I had 15 wonderful years. He died in 1985.

MATCHMAKER MAVIS. Author is all smiles as a bride in 1970, thanks to "the second Mavis" (at right) who introduced her to husband Joe.

I'll never forget the two Mavises who so profoundly influenced my life. I have two stepchildren, three grandchildren and so many wonderful memories thanks to these good friends.

Mail Carrier Delivered Some Sound Advice

By Winnifred Hanson, Grapeland, Texas

THE ADVICE I received from my mailman, Johnny, back in 1957 changed my life forever.

One day, Johnny lingered near my mailbox as I went to get the mail. He suggested I come along with him to learn the route. He'd be retiring soon and thought I'd make a good replacement.

"I'm too old," I balked. "I'm 57!"

"No, you're not too old," Johnny replied.

Well, Johnny finally convinced me, and I learned to case the mail, get the package notices in the right places and efficiently cover a route of 400 families.

I carried this route for 15 years, retiring when I was 72. Not once did I receive a complaint about leaving mail at an improper location. It was a great job that gave me a good retirement. Today, I'm well over 90 and feel great.

But the best honor of all was that I was the first woman mail carrier in the whole state of Texas.

Mechanic's Boss Helped Him Shift Career into High Gear

By Wilfred Tritz, Waukesha, Wisconsin

MY FIRST JOB after World War II was as an auto mechanic. Back then there were very few special tools or fixtures to make the job easier, so I designed and built many of my own.

One day, the owner of the dealership called me into his office. "Bill," he said, "you show a remarkable propensity for design engineering. Why don't you go back to school and get an engineering degree? I know you can do it. The GI Bill will help pay for it. Go to night school if necessary."

I thought my career choice had been the right one, until that conversation.

I enrolled in night school and a correspondence course. It wasn't easy, but 6 years later I was a full-fledged mechanical engineer. My first job was designing hydraulic units for auto body repair.

Later, I was hired by an engine manufacturer and eventually became the plant engineer—all because someone recognized potential I didn't know I had.

MECHANICALLY INCLINED Wilfred Tritz, as he appeared in 1942. He didn't know it then, but a wise tip would send him in the right direction.

I'm now retired, but often think about the man who had faith in my abilities. I wish I had the opportunity to thank him, but he has gone on to his reward.

6-Year-Old Made Mother Rethink Her Priorities

By Cathy Weber-Zunker, Alexandria, Minnesota

WHEN my oldest son was in first grade, our morning ritual was to walk across the street together and wait for his school bus. This was our special private time to kick rocks, play in the leaves or snow—whatever entertainment the season afforded us.

I own and operate a daycare center, and one morning, a parent arrived early while John and I were waiting for the bus. I told John I'd go back across the street and wave to him from the front porch. He said that was fine.

As the parent was talking to me about her schedule for the day, I turned and saw John's bus pulling away. My heart sank. I had missed it, our moment together.

I kept telling myself that I was the one who was upset, John probably didn't even notice. How wrong I was.

AS A GRADE-SCHOOLER, young John taught his mother a valuable lesson that she has never forgotten. Sometimes the wisdom from children is the best we can follow.

A few minutes later, John called me from school. He wasn't crying, but he sounded like he had a frog in his throat. "Mom," he said, "you were too busy with your daycare kids, and you didn't wave to me!"

I apologized to John. Then I called my husband at work and asked him to come home and take over the daycare because I had to go to school. I went to the playground, found that 6-year-old boy, got down on my knees so we were eyeball to eyeball and apologized.

That one statement made me stop and look at my life, my priorities, my children. I needed to always make my own children feel special and to rearrange my activities so I had time to become friends with them.

Many thanks to that 6-year-old who said exactly what I needed to hear all those years ago. It changed my life forever.

Chapter Three

What a
Lucky Break!

The Farmer Takes a Wife...
On Nationwide Television

By Mary Kershner, Findlay, Ohio

HOWARD and I had a blind date on May 6, 1951 and liked each other from the start. By the spring of 1952, we were sure we wanted to get married.

In May, Howard's mother wrote to the *Bride & Groom* TV show, in hopes we could get married on the air. Howard's father was sick and couldn't leave the house for our wedding, but he could see it if we got married on television.

In July, Howard received a letter and application form with questions about how we met, where we went on dates and our likes and dislikes.

At the end of August, we received a telegram saying we'd be on *Bride & Groom* October 1! Howard was the first farmer who'd ever applied, and that was one reason we were chosen.

We left Findlay, Ohio on Friday, September 27. It was my 20th birthday. We spent that night in Pennsylvania and reached our hotel in New York City the next afternoon.

Even Supplied the Gown

On Monday, we toured the TV studio, met everyone connected with the program and got our marriage license. On Tuesday, we had rehearsals, and I was fitted for a wedding gown from the show's wardrobe department.

On Wednesday, we returned to the studio at 9 a.m. for another rehearsal. By the time we got into our wedding clothes and makeup, it was time for Howard and Mary to get married on *Bride & Groom*. The ceremony ran from noon to 12:15, including commercials. Our wedding was sponsored by Betty Crocker.

Afterward we received our gifts—two pieces of farm machinery, wedding rings, luggage, a stove, silverware, an iron and a toaster. Then we were given a rental car and sent on our wedding trip—a 5-night, all-expenses-paid stay at Hidden Valley Ranch near Lake Luzerne, New York.

Because our wedding was televised, most of the people in our hometowns were able to see it. The furniture store where my dad worked even closed down that day so his fellow employees could go see Howard on TV. Everyone went to nearby stores that sold televisions so they could watch.

THE WHOLE NATION was invited to Howard and Mary Kershner's wedding! They were married in 1952 on television's popular program, *Bride & Groom.* Maybe you recall "attending" their ceremony.

Shortage of Parking Spaces Opened Up Job Opportunity

By Mary Mertens, Sterling, Colorado

IN 1939, I graduated from college with a degree in education. Summer was coming to a close, and I hadn't found a job, so I started visiting neighboring county courthouses to ask about teaching positions.

One day, my parents came along and dropped me off at a courthouse while they looked for a parking space. The school superintendent told me she didn't know of any openings, so I left.

When I reached the parking lot, I didn't see my parents' car, so I walked to the end of the block. Still no car.

As I walked back toward the courthouse, the superintendent's secretary came running toward me. "Just after you left, three school board members came in saying they were looking for a teacher," she said.

I went back in to talk with the board members. The job was at a one-room schoolhouse with 15 students. I not only took the

SHE LANDED A JOB. Mary Mertens looks mighty pleased in 1940, her first full year as a teacher.

job, but married the son of one of the board members!

We've been married over 50 years and have five children, 18 grandchildren and two great-grandchildren—all because there was no parking space in front of the courthouse!

This Lucky Break Was No Accident

By John Cappleman, Childress, Texas

SUDDENLY, I was wide awake and racing toward a grove of trees.

It was spring of 1973, and I was on a long drive from Houston to San Antonio, Texas. I'd been lulled into a deep sleep for a few seconds and snapped awake. Headed toward those trees at 65 miles an hour, I knew my chances of survival were slim. Every muscle in my body tensed in panic.

In less than 3 seconds, it was all over. My car had stopped just 5 feet short of 12 majestic live oak trees. How could a 2,000-pound car stop on its own?

Spring in the Texas Hill Country means bluebonnets—and lots of them. They were growing so thickly that year, they literally wrapped around all four of my tires and pulled me to a complete stop.

Today, I owe my life to God...and the Texas bluebonnets.

Sheltered from Storm, They Found Each Other

By Mildred Mueting, Axtell, Kansas

SEVERAL of my husband's ancestors came to the United States from Germany in 1885. His grandmother, Katherine, followed in 1896 and moved in with a sister and her family in Kansas.

That spring, a typical Kansas storm came up, and Katherine and other family members took refuge in a storm cellar. A young man named Herman Mueting was traveling along the road when the storm hit, and he took shelter along with them. Herman and Katherine were married a few months later.

Kansas is known for its tornadoes, but to our family, this storm had a beautiful silver lining.

Fate Kept Immigrants Off Ill-Fated Ship

By Sandy Hall, Plainfield, Wisconsin

EARLY this century, Gustaf Dedeyne came to the United States to explore a possible new life for himself and his bride, Emily. With hard work, he saved enough money to return to Belgium so he could bring Emily back to the States.

LUCKY VOYAGERS Gustaf and Emily Dedeyne, before they left Belgium for America.

When he arrived in Belgium, he was delighted to discover that many of their cousins had booked passage to the U.S., too. Gustaf and Emily tried to exchange their tickets so they would all be on the same boat, to no avail. They were forced to travel by themselves.

They later realized a guardian angel had been watching over them. All but one of their cousins was lost on the trip. They were passengers on the maiden voyage of the *Titanic*.

Emily and Gustaf arrived safely and began a family that now stretches from the East Coast to the West. They are my husband's grandparents, and though they aren't directly related to me, my life would be much different if they had been able to exchange their tickets.

LUCKY LYDIA, third from right, with American coworkers, 1914.

Storm-Tossed Sea Kept Her Out of Harm's Way

By Vi Lien, Mesa, Arizona

A STORM at sea was a lucky break for my mother—and all of her descendants.

Lydia Gustafson was booked to sail for America on the "unsinkable" *Titanic* in 1912. She said a tearful good-bye to her parents, brothers and sister, then left her native Sweden on a ship for England.

A severe storm in the North Sea delayed her ship, and by the time Lydia reached England, the *Titanic* had already sailed.

Lydia was rebooked on another ship, the *Mauretania*. She was sailing aboard that ship on April 14, when the captain addressed the passengers with this somber announcement: "We just heard an SOS call, but we are too far away to help. The sinking ship is the *Titanic*."

Discarded Letter Led to 60-Plus Years of Marriage

By Diana Clark, Decatur, Illinois

AT 16, Grandma Cleta lived in Texas with her very popular older sister, who had many pen pals. One day, Cleta's sister decided she'd received "one letter too many" from a young man in Illinois and threw his letter on the wood pile.

Cleta retrieved it and began corresponding with John. They developed a lively long-distance friendship through their letters—until the last one. John wrote, "Cleta, don't answer this letter, 'cause I'm on my way to Texas to marry you." They had five children, 10 grandchildren and enjoyed more than 60 years together.

Chance Meeting Turned Old Pals into Newlyweds

By Al Armbruster, Geneva, Illinois

WHILE working as a school crossing guard, I recognized a woman I hadn't seen in years. As we talked, she told me her husband had died within the past year.

Later that week, I impulsively went to her house and asked if I could mow the lawn or do something to help her. She seemed surprised, but pitched in as I helped trim bushes and haul branches to the curb. I left wondering what I should do next to get closer to this beautiful woman.

I didn't have to do anything. She knocked on my door and asked me to accompany her to a party. She had no lack of escorts, but wanted a "reliable friendly neighbor" she could trust. I wasn't sure that description fit, as I was becoming dazzled by this woman.

After that, I planned outings and cooked dinner when she had night classes at college. We traveled, danced, laughed and talked—all the usual courtship rituals. The day after she received her graduate degree, the lady became my wife. I've often wondered what would have happened if Barbara hadn't appeared on my corner. Our meeting there was indeed my lucky break.

BROUGHT TOGETHER on a busy street was this couple. As a school crossing guard, Al worked the busiest corner in town, making chance encounter possible.

Madison County's Bridges Reunited Childhood Pals

By Bonnie Songer, Winterset, Iowa

I WAS BORN and raised in Madison County, Iowa, home of the covered bridges in *The Bridges of Madison County*. I never dreamed what fame and fortune those bridges would bring our community, or the role they would play in a special friendship.

In January 1953, my family moved to Arizona to help ease my father's lung problems. Our next-door neighbors were an American-Indian family, and I became best friends with their daughter, Verna. We were together every day, spending as much time together as possible.

In late March, homesick and low on cash, my folks decided to return to the farm. It was a sad day when I said

BRIDGED BY FRIENDSHIP. Bonnie (left) and Verna hadn't seen each other in 43 years. A lucky break in the form of a movie ticket got them back together.

good-bye to Verna, but we corresponded nearly every other week for about 20 years.

In the early 1970s, Verna moved to San Francisco, and I lost track of her. All of my letters were returned. This was a real loss, but I knew it would take a great force to keep us from communicating. She must have passed away.

In the summer of 1995, I had a shock. The phone rang— and it was Verna! I could hardly believe my ears. She'd lost my address when she moved to San Francisco. So how did she find me? *The Bridges of Madison County* jogged her memory!

During the movie, Meryl Streep mentions Winterset, and Verna remembered that was my hometown. She saw the movie a second time to look for more clues. Then she remembered I had a brother named Dan. She called directory assistance to get his number in Winterset, and he gave her my number.

I couldn't believe we were talking again after 43 years! We laughed and cried as we updated each other on our families.

In mid-July, Verna called again. She had a birthday coming up, and the only gift she wanted was to see me again. Since Madison County's bridges had brought us back together, she wanted to see them with me.

When Verna got off the plane in Des Moines that September, the last 43 years melted away in a mist. We hadn't seen each other since we were 13 years old, but time seemed to stop for us. What a lucky break for both of us that she'd gone to see that movie.

I look at our familiar covered bridges in a new way now, for they brought Verna and me back together after all these years.

She Took Exam on a Lark, But Job Offer Was No Joke

By Alice Mason, Toledo, Iowa

IN 1942, during my summer break from Clarion State College in Pennsylvania, I visited relatives in Iowa. When my cousin took the state teacher's exams, I took them too, just to see if I could pass.

On the way back to Pennsylvania, I stopped in Wisconsin to visit friends and received a call from Iowa. I had passed the exams and was being offered a teaching job at $70 a month!

This was during World War II and there was a shortage of teachers. Instead of returning for my senior year of college, I moved to Iowa and taught at a country school. At the end of that first school year, I married a young farmer. We enjoyed 34 years together and had six children.

THE OLD COLLEGE TRY? It resulted in an "early out" from college for Alice Mason, seen here in 1942.

Friend's Visit Canceled Plans for Plane Trip

By Irene Horst, Tappen, North Dakota

ONE WEEKEND I wanted to fly from Great Falls, Montana to visit my boyfriend in Spokane, Washington. My roommate's boyfriend was flying to that area with a friend and told me I was welcome to come along.

I was all set to go when a good friend from Alabama arrived unexpectedly. Johnny was on his way to a job in Alaska and had made a special trip just to see me. I felt I owed it to him to cancel my trip to Spokane.

The next day, my roommate called me at work. Her boyfriend's plane had crashed in the mountains near Helena and there were no survivors. Johnny saved my life when he asked me to stay home.

Lost Little Boys Knew Who They Were, Not Where

By Louise Smith, Springfield, Illinois

MY GRANDFATHER often told me stories about his childhood in the hills of southern Illinois, near Shawnee National Forest. This is one of my favorites.

One afternoon, he and his brother went fishing. They were about 8 and 9 at the time and knew they had to be home by dark to do chores before supper.

The sun was sinking as they gathered their bamboo poles and coffee can of worms, so they decided to take a shortcut through Old Man Hatcher's woods. They could get to the meadow on the other side before dark, when Old Man Hatcher turned his dogs loose.

Before they knew it, they were deep in the woods, and it had become pitch dark. Old Man Hatcher's dogs were howling. The younger boy started to whimper, and the older one tried to console him. They were lost.

The older boy suggested they climb a tree. He boosted his little brother up, following closely behind. Now it was getting foggy. They couldn't see the moon or stars. They were tired, cold, scared, hungry and trying hard not to cry.

Spooky Sounds Echoed

Then they heard a low sound. "Whooo!" What was that? It sounded so clear. "Whooo! Whooo!" Without hesitating, both boys replied, "Tom and John, Pa's boys." The mysterious voice called again, "Whooo!" The boys said, a little louder, "Tom and John, Pa's boys."

Back at the farm, Ma raced to the barn for Pa when the boys didn't respond to her calls or the supper gong. She

GIDDYAP! Little Louise Smith was rarin' to ride on "Pop's" old plow horse. Pop was Louise's grandfather, and she cherishes memories of him today.

was frantic—this wasn't like them. Pa stopped milking the cow, hitched up the horses and took the buckboard to the neighbor's. He'd need help searching for the boys.

Soon a group of townsfolk had gathered with lanterns, torches and dogs to guide them through the dark foggy night. Some took wagons to the river to look along the banks. Others searched the path leading to the road. Pa went with a third group into the woods.

After about 200 yards, the group stopped in its tracks. "Whooo! Whooo!" Then came a faint, "Tom and John, Pa's boys." They couldn't believe it! They listened closely. There it was again. "Whooo! Whooo!" "Tom and John, Pa's boys."

More Scared Than Ever

As the group moved toward the voices, Tom and John heard rustling. They feared it was Old Man Hatcher's dogs—or, worse, a bobcat or bear. They yelled louder and louder in response to each "Whooo!" Maybe they could scare off whatever was making that rustling noise.

When the searchers spotted the boys, Pa broke into an excited run. The boys were clinging to branches in the middle of the tree. When they saw Pa, they were so happy they jumped into his waiting arms.

At the farm, Ma greeted Pa and the boys with tears streaming down her face and caught the three of them in a tight hug. She fixed the boys warm milk and heated up their forgotten meal—beef stew, biscuits and apple dumplings.

After thanking each neighbor personally and shaking his hand, Pa joined his little family for a midnight supper. Once he and Ma had put the boys to bed and thanked God for their return, he told her about the owl's call and the boys' response.

They shared a quiet laugh together. But what Pa didn't say was that those calls were probably the only thing that led the rescuers to the boys…one of whom turned out to be my grandfather, who many years later, enjoyed telling me the story.

Was Perfect Home a Stroke Of Luck…or Meant To Be?

By Nona Van Os, Hannibal, Missouri

TWO YEARS AGO, my husband was about to retire, and I was looking for an apartment for us. One stormy morning, I happened to be on the phone with my sister, and I told

her it wasn't a good day for apartment hunting. But as soon as we hung up, I felt absolutely compelled to go.

My first stop was at a realty company. A nice lady there said they didn't list apartment rentals, but she wrote two names on a slip of paper and said I could call from there.

I dialed the first number. The woman who answered said she'd been trying to find her glasses so she could call the very office I was standing in to list her property. It was

BORN IN A BARN? Nope. But Nona Van Os is thrilled to live in one now. This converted dairy barn and attached silo is her dream home. What a lucky break to find it!

a converted dairy barn with an attached silo—just what I wanted!

Was it luck, or was it meant to be? I say it's the latter. This home is perfect for us.

Berlin Wall Halted Her
Plan to Teach in Germany

By Ann Marie Wollenberg, Canal Winchester, Ohio

IN FALL of 1960, I heard some local teachers had spent 2 years teaching American children in foreign countries. I was single and had never been away from home. It sounded exciting to teach in a foreign land and travel around Europe during school breaks.

I applied for one of the jobs and was accepted in the spring of 1961. I quit my teaching job in Youngstown, Ohio and requested an assignment in Germany.

That summer, turmoil broke out in Berlin and elsewhere in Germany. As they listened to the news reports, my parents feared for my life. What if I was sent to Berlin?

When the Berlin Wall was erected, I grew uneasy, too. I still didn't know where I was being sent. I decided to back out. Luckily, I was able to get my job back in Youngstown.

The next school year, I moved to Columbus, Ohio. Four years later, I met my husband, with whom I have three grown children.

Who knows—if I'd accepted that overseas assignment, I might have married a German native and stayed there. Instead I'm married to a wonderful man of German descent.

'Older Woman' Set Up Teen
Admirer With Her Sister

By Sherry Masters, Cincinnati, Ohio

IN 1957, my sister Janie worked in the accounting department of a chemical company. She was attractive and vivacious, and every available man in the office wanted to date her.

Bob Masters had just been promoted to the accounting department, and he worked right next to Janie. He asked her to go out numerous times before she finally said yes.

A few days before their date, Janie learned Bob was only 17. She was a lady of 21. She broke the date, but told Bob she had a 16-year-old sister. That's how Bob and I came to have a blind date at the drive-in. We were married 2-1/2 years later.

HAPPY COUPLE Bob and Sherry Masters wouldn't have met had Sherry's sister not learned Bob's age and suggested he date a younger "alternate".

Wife's Influence Transformed Carnival Worker into Preacher

By John Belderes
Pittsville, Virginia

MY DAD and I made our living working at carnivals. I was a "carny".

In 1946, after my discharge from the Army, I found myself in the hospital and fell head over heels in love with a student nurse. What she saw in me, I'll never know. But Someone somewhere had a hand in this union.

MIDWAY TO HEAVEN. As a 17-year-old in 1940, John Belderes worked as a carny. He later took the pulpit and served as a pastor.

We married after a whirlwind courtship, and I took her to Florida. I didn't want her to be part of the carnival lifestyle.

Life was hard. I remember working all week for $29. But we were blessed with four wonderful children.

The one thing my wife insisted on was that she and the kids go to church every Sunday. By then we'd bought a small country grocery store. My wife couldn't drive, so every Sunday I closed the store, took my family to church, came back to open the store, then returned to bring them home.

One day, my oldest son said, "Dad, I'm not going to church anymore." When I asked why, he said, "Because you don't go."

Well, I loved my family so much that I started to go. In time, I joined the church. Later, I became a Gideon, speaking and placing Bibles in motels, hospitals, schools and other locations.

In 1972, we returned to Virginia and joined the local church. The people there knew I was a Gideon and asked me to preach. I did. Then they asked me to become their pastor, because they had none. I said no. I already had a job promised to me.

Then my wife got sick. She was in the hospital for 4 days. I walked the halls and drank a hundred cups of coffee, hoping and praying she'd get well.

Finally I realized what the Lord wanted. With tears in my eyes, I surrendered to the call and began at age 50.

Today, I'm 72 and retired from the active ministry, but still preaching. I've pastored three churches and made thousands of friends, and life has never been so wonderful.

Stranded Sawmill Employee Found Work—and a Wife

By Charles Clark, Ransomville, New York

MY MOTHER was born and raised in the "fruit country" of western New York. After her mother's death, she was taken in by a well-to-do family of fruit farmers and stayed with them as a domestic.

My dad grew up in Ohio and went to work at a sawmill in Michigan after graduating from high school. When the timber company needed men to build another mill in the Adirondacks of New York, Dad volunteered and was put on a train with several other men.

Dad couldn't sleep on the train, so when he learned they'd have an 8-hour layover in Buffalo, New York, he got off and checked into a hotel. The desk clerk was instructed to call Dad an hour before the train was supposed to leave.

The call came, and Dad walked across the street to the station. He found no train there! It had pulled out 2 hours earlier. There he was, stranded in a strange city with very little money.

Someone suggested he go to Niagara County where he could get a job picking apples. Dad had enough money to board a bus and ended up working at the same farm as my mother. He never made it to the Adirondacks.

Job Opportunity Was Nearly Tossed Aside

By Eleanor Taylor, Westbrook, Maine

IN 1957, I answered an ad for a stenographer at a small Ohio manufacturing company. After an interview, I was told the company had several other applicants, and I'd be advised.

When I carried in the mail several days later, I sorted out the junk mail to throw in the trash. One envelope in the junk pile was decorated with the outline of a bus. I figured it was an advertisement for a bus tour.

As I flipped the pile into the trash basket, the bus envelope turned over, revealing the manufacturing company's name on the back flap. It was a letter asking me to come in for a second interview. (That's when I discovered the company made equipment for city and school buses.)

I got the stenographer's job, and I grew with the company, moving up from secretarial work to positions that previously had been held only by men. I worked many years in sales and production control and retired in 1985 after 28 years.

THANKS, MR. POSTMAN! Had postal miscues not happened, this wedding wouldn't have, either.

Two Lost Letters Helped Her Find Her Dream

By Mary Ellen Brown
Pittsfield, New Hampshire

I DREAMED of going to college when I grew up. It would be my escape, a way to make a better life for myself.

As I was growing up, I moved too many times to count and attended numerous schools, but I worked hard and got good grades.

During my senior year in 1970, I was suddenly homeless. Thankfully, a farm family with eight children was willing to take me in. I worked for my room and board.

This family was kind and generous, but it was obvious their meager food was being stretched to accommodate me. I had to find a job and a place to live. I had been accepted at the University of Maine, but even with several scholarships, I was far short of the needed tuition.

I found an inexpensive apartment in Penacook, New Hampshire and had just enough money for the first week's rent. Jobs were scarce. A factory agreed to hire me—on one condition.

"We don't want to train you only to have you leave in the fall," the personnel director told me. "If you withdraw from college and show me the letter, I'll hire you."

The Rent Was Due

I was stunned, but had no other choice. The next day, I brought him the letter asking the college to withdraw me. I mailed it that day and began work.

Boring doesn't begin to describe that summer. Sometimes I was glad I used a large microscope in my work, because it hid my face as the tears fell. My dream was gone. My income was barely enough to pay for rent and food. I was stuck, going nowhere.

The last week of August, a letter arrived with several forwarding addresses from my previous residences, each crossed out and leading to another. It was from the university.

My hands trembled as I tore open the envelope, sure it was just a late response to my withdrawal. But soon I was jumping up and down with excitement.

What Was the News?

"You've been awarded a grant and work-study program," the letter said. With my scholarships, I had more than enough money for the first semester.

Afraid it wasn't true, I went to a pay phone and called the administration office. "Did you get a letter from me in June that said I wasn't coming?" I asked.

The lady on the phone checked and said no.

"So this is true? I've been awarded a Pell Grant, and you're still expecting me?"

"That's right. Don't forget, classes start next week."

On Monday morning, I went to the personnel director's office and handed him the letter. He read it and sat silently. I showed him all the forwarding addresses.

"I mailed the letter I showed you," I assured him. "I don't know what happened. Maybe it got lost."

He stood and reached out to shake my hand. "Guess I can't stand in the way of this," he said, smiling. "Good luck."

I didn't have enough money for bus fare to Maine, but some friends knew a young man who was driving there, and he agreed to drop me off. I chattered and smiled the whole way. The nice young man helped me find my dorm room and said good-bye.

A few weeks later, he called and asked me on a date. You guessed it—we fell in love and eventually married.

He still laughs when he tells our children about the day he took me to college. Who knows what would've happened if that first letter hadn't been lost, and that second letter hadn't been forwarded so tenaciously?

Chapter Four

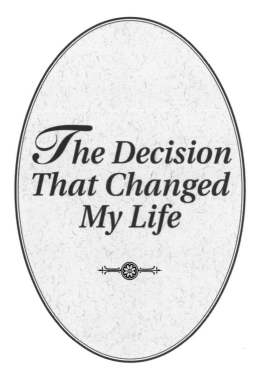

Mother Never Gave Up Child... And Child Never Gave Up on Her

By Genevieve Ingraham
San Francisco, California

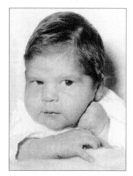

BABY MARGO at 1 month. Mom's tough decision paid off for both mother and child.

BACK IN 1954, I found myself alone with three small children—and another on the way. My husband had left me, I was living on public assistance and had no idea how to manage with a fourth child.

Well-meaning friends and neighbors urged me to give up the child for adoption. In my heart of hearts, I didn't want to. But my oldest was only 5, and I had 3-year-old twins. Would it be fair to them to bring another child home? Just caring for three overwhelmed me at times.

I spent long hours praying, asking God to help me make the right choice. Sadly, I made my decision. When the baby was born, I would contact Social Services and surrender the child.

I went into labor late on a Saturday night, when the Social Services Department was closed for the weekend. When my beautiful baby girl was born the next morning, I just couldn't find the words to give her up. I named her Margo. What a blessing she has been to me!

I'm now 79, with multiple disabilities. When my health took a turn for the worse, Margo moved me to her apartment building.

She now does my cooking, cleaning, laundry, errands and takes me to my doctor appointments—all while attending school full-time. She also schedules me for physical therapy, activities at the senior center and for monthly outings with an organization that assists wheelchair users.

I love all my children, but it's the one I nearly gave up who refused to let my life slip away.

'Our Widowed Parents Married Each Other!'

By Laura Gran, Ashtabula, Ohio

TWO WEDDINGS resulted when Laura and Carl met. Above, they pose with widowed parents Arminta and Merle. One year later (below), the parents were wed.

THE DECISION that changed my life forever and for the better did the same thing for three other people.

I was going to college in my hometown of Ashtabula, Ohio. I had planned to move out of state—a new job, new home, new college—but as the date drew closer, I just couldn't leave my family behind.

Instead, I stayed in Ashtabula and continued attending the same community college. That's where I met my future husband, Carl.

Before we were married in 1988, each of us lost a parent—my dad in 1987 and Carl's mom just before our wedding. My mom and Carl's dad danced at our wedding, and the rest is history. On July 15, 1989, our widowed parents married each other.

The gatherings for our large extended family are a lot of fun because we all get along so well. I can't imagine my life any other way.

And our sadness at losing two parents in such a short span of time has been eased by the happiness our

surviving parents have found with each other.

Who would have known that so many lives would be touched by my decision not to move?

Lost-at-Sea WAC Found Her Bearings Through Story

By Enid Treffinger, Federal Way, Washington

I'VE often wondered what course my life would have taken if one of its weeks hadn't held two Tuesdays.

It was November 1945, and I was cruising home from Manila on the *SS Lurline*, a former luxury

STEAMING HOME. In fall of 1945, Enid Treffinger was all smiles before departing Manila aboard the troopship, *SS Lurline*.

liner turned troopship. Aboard were 500 other members of the Women's Army Corps.

I was completely at sea—in more ways than one. After 3 eventful years in the Army, I still didn't know what to do with my life.

All of us were impatient to be home and tried to make the days speed by. We played bridge, relaxed on deck and watched the flying fish and sea snakes. I gazed at the wake impatiently, willing the waters to part more swiftly. The 2-week journey seemed interminable.

To make matters worse, one of those weeks had two Tuesdays because of our passage over the International Date Line. On that second Tuesday, I was bored with bridge games and lolling, so I borrowed *Anna and the King of Siam* from the ship's library.

Became Absorbed in Story

I immediately lost myself in the story of Anna Owens, the English governess at the court of Siam. One of her pupils was the future king, and Anna taught him that all men had a right to freedom and liberty. When he ascended the throne, one of his first acts was to free the slaves who were held in his kingdom.

The book's central truth excited me. One woman, through her teaching, had influenced the course of history!

For the first time in my life, I fully realized what a force for good education could be. Distressed by the war just ended, I realized the only hope for eliminating war and its horrors lay in education.

Suddenly I knew what do with my life. I spent the next 5 years studying to become a teacher and then taught for 30 years.

That book, and those two Tuesdays, gave my life a direction I was grateful to follow. I may not have changed the course of history as Anna Owens did, but I did what I could to help the cause of peace in the world.

Decision to Attend Operetta Led to Lifelong Love

By Harry Buskirk
Augusta, Kansas

WAGON LOAD OF SMILES. Pauline and Harry Buskirk had fun posing for this photo in July, 1938.

BACK IN 1938, my friend Clifford and I were restless 20-year-olds in our small hometown in Kansas. One night we were wondering what to do in our "dumb ole" town when Clifford suggested we go to the high school operetta.

That was the *last thing* I wanted to do, but we decided to go anyway.

The prettiest girl I'd ever seen was singing the lead, and I fell for her. After the program, I asked her if she was new in town, because I'd never seen her before. Turned out she'd lived only a few blocks from me most of her life—but then she was 3 years younger.

I soon lost track of Clifford. I was too busy dating, falling in love and marrying that beautiful girl. I still thank God for directing me to her...I really should write to Clifford and thank him for dragging me to that operetta!

Senior's Last-Minute Class Switch Was Just His Type

By Charles Martin, Bartlesville, Oklahoma

BACK DURING MY senior year of high school, I needed one more class to graduate and hurriedly chose woodworking.

The first day I spent in that class, I knew I'd made a mistake.

The instructor said the class was at capacity. Would one of us consider dropping out to make room for another very interested student? I did—and ended up in a typing class.

Typing! I shuddered at the thought. But it wasn't that difficult, and I probably learned more than I would have in woodworking.

Three years later, while serving in the military, my commanding officer asked if any of us knew how to type. I stepped forward. Soon I was named company clerk, with a promotion to corporal. I was elated.

My typing skills relieved me of many other drudge assignments. Later, when we went overseas for World War II, my position as company clerk kept me away from some of the hazards—but all of us in our unit faced some frightening times.

After my discharge, I was hired by an oil company to type important documents. Later on, my job didn't require typing, but I remained with that company nearly 40 years until retirement.

I've often wondered if it was just coincidence that I dropped woodworking and enrolled in that typing class so long ago. Who knows where some of these impulsive decisions come from, and why they lead us where they do.

An Act of Thanks Started Family on Path to America

By Lili Idnurm, Painesville, Ohio

IN 1948, I was 16 years old and living with my family in a displaced persons' camp in Germany. We had fled our native Estonia in 1944 during the Russian occupation.

FUTURE CITIZEN of the U.S., Lili Idnurm, as she appeared in Germany in 1948.

Then one day my Brownie troop received a package of combs, toothbrushes, pencils and other items from a Girl Scout troop in Painesville, Ohio. The senders' names and addresses were in the box, and since I knew English, I sent them a heart-felt thank-you note. This led to a wonderful correspondence.

The girls took my letters to their Sunday school teacher, Fred Volk, who in turn began writing to me. Soon he was looking for a sponsor so my family could emigrate to the United States.

On July 21, 1949, my parents, brother and I arrived in Painesville, and it has become our home. My husband, also an Estonian, and I raised our three children here and have found many nice friends.

All this for sending a thank-you note! You never know when a small decision in your life will change it completely.

Blind Date Changed Their Lives Forever

By Joy Price
Midlothian, Texas

LOVE AT FIRST FLIGHT. Airman Don Price and wife Joy felt love take wing on their first date—made possible by Joy's abrupt decision.

IT WAS a Friday night in 1963, and I was a junior at North Texas State University in Denton. Most of the other girls on my dormitory floor had gone home for the weekend or were out on dates.

I was sitting there alone in my room, wondering what to do when I heard a girl walking up and down the hall asking if anyone wanted a date that night.

I'd never met the girl before. She said her date had come down from Altus Air Force base in Oklahoma with a tall good-looking buddy, and they needed a date for him. That sounded interesting to me, so I decided to go along.

When I came home that night, I told my roommate I'd met the man I was going to marry. She laughed and went back to sleep. Don proposed 3 weeks later, and we married June 20. Yes, it was truly love at first sight.

But there's more to this story. A friend of mine dated one of Don's coworkers, who was always asking Don to go with him to Denton to meet "a girl who'd be perfect for him". They tried several times, but were never able to leave the base at the same time.

After our first date, Don returned to base and told his buddy about the wonderful girl he'd met. His friend nearly fainted. *I* was the girl he'd wanted Don to meet!

I truly believe our marriage was made in heaven.

Going to College Turned Single Mom's Life Around

By Nona May Van Os, Hannibal, Missouri

"WOULD YOU like to go to college? We think you'd make a great teacher."

Suddenly the old milk can I was using for a chair felt like a royal throne. I peered across the kitchen at my preacher friends, O.L. and Bill, and gave them a resounding "Yes"! Never mind the minor details; it would all work out. I knew that in my heart.

It was 1964, and I was a single parent with six children ages 1 to 11. I loved them dearly and wanted a better life for them. But my assets were meager. All I had was an old 1953 Chevrolet. O.L. and Bill were the answer to my prayers.

Two weeks later, Bill drove me to Central Missouri State University, where I filled out some papers. Then he presented my case at the financial aid office. The man behind the desk was nice but skeptical.

"Umm, six children?" he asked. He wondered how I thought I could do this. They'd never had a single mother of six as a student before. I pleaded for a chance to prove myself and promised to work hard.

When I walked out of the office with the assurance of a loan, I was thrilled. It was as though all my problems had been solved.

Kids Helped, Too

When I got home, I sat my children in a circle and explained that they would have to help as much as they could. They took this very seriously and did as much housework as their ages would allow. My sisters baby-sat for the boys while my daughters were in school.

From 1964 to 1967, I went to college each fall and spring and took winter and summer off to spend with the children. In 1965, O.L. introduced me to a man, and we married after a 2-year courtship.

In May 1971, my husband, relatives and six happy children applauded as I received my bachelor's degree in elementary education. My oldest daughter had just graduated from high school.

BETTER TIMES AHEAD. Mom, Nona May, returned to school to help Steve, Clint, Joy, Donna, Nona and Linda.

I loved teaching, and one of my children followed in my footsteps, teaching fifth grade. Four of the six have college degrees, and four served their country. I'm proud of them all.

I'm thankful that O.L. and Bill believed in my ability to overcome obstacles and forge ahead—and glad that they saw the glass half-full.

Friend's Suggestion Launched Housewife on Teaching Career

By Elverda Carlock, Montrose, Missouri

WHEN a preschool opened in our community, a friend encouraged me to apply to work as a teacher. I baby-sat for her, and she said I'd be perfect in such a position because I was so good with kids.

My husband and I had agreed long ago that I'd stay home and raise our four daughters while he earned a living. But this would only be 3 hours a day, 3 blocks from home. This job seemed a heaven-sent opportunity. I decided to try for it.

I got the position and received on-the-job training, which included some college classes in early childhood education. Within a few years, I was appointed director of a Head-start center.

At age 46, I graduated from college and was offered the first teaching position I applied for. I taught kindergarten for 18 years.

Now retired, I'm still amazed that I—a shy woman whose only ambition was to be a good mother—could have had such a successful satisfying career.

Layoff Sped Up the Right Decision

By Taryn Simpson, Lebanon, Tennessee

I HAD already made up my mind to move from the city to the country. I just couldn't figure out how or when it would happen.

I was a personnel manager in Houston, Texas and was weary of seeing nothing but buildings and concrete every day. Just driving to work was exhausting.

But I couldn't just leave a good job and land in Small Town, USA without another job—it was too chancy. And, yet, I couldn't ignore the urge to move to the country. I felt like I was holding my breath. I needed to exhale.

In March 1994, I made up my mind. I was moving. All I needed was a plan. I considered several New England states, but the cost of living was too expensive. Then my sister suggested Tennessee and encouraged me to think about Nashville.

I sent for brochures and decided to visit Nashville during my vacation in May. I even began budgeting to move there in a year or two, although I still felt guilty about leaving a good job.

At the end of April, my boss gave me some bad news. The office was being dissolved. I had to lay off everyone but the accounting department.

Faced a Tough Day

That Friday was one of the toughest days of my life. I laid off single mothers, people living paycheck to paycheck—and I suspected there was more to come.

The following Monday, the other shoe dropped. The rest of us were given 2 months' notice of layoff. My decision was made for me. I was moving to Tennessee.

I put my house up for sale, began packing and started looking for an apartment. My head was swimming with anxiety. I was finally going to Nashville, and I'd never even been there!

I rented a grimy duplex in Antioch, Tennessee. For exactly

A HOME IN THE COUNTRY was waiting for Taryn Simpson, when the decision to move was forced on her by job loss. Had she not been laid off, she'd likely never have found this home of her dreams.

one year, my mother, our two hound dogs and I lived in 800 square feet of mildew while I looked for work. I spent Sundays flipping through the classifieds and applied for every job in my field and then some. I began to wonder if I'd made the right decision.

But I'm a stubborn cuss, and I had a dream—a good job and a home on acreage with lots of scenery. At times I thought I'd go crazy, but I was determined to get my prize.

After 10 months, I was offered a good job with a travel center on Music Row. I made an offer on the house of my dreams, and it was accepted.

One evening as I sat on a lawn chair, looking at our beautiful backyard and adjoining pond, I realized that for the first time since I'd left Houston, I was able to exhale. I guess the moral of my story is: Never give up on a dream. You may be closer to it than you think.

Pen Pal Program Led Iowa Teen to 'Swedish Sister'

By Linda Burkgren
Clear Lake, Iowa

BACK IN 1967, I never would've thought that 25¢ would bring me happiness, travel and a pen pal who would become as dear as a sister.

It all began when my freshman English teacher suggested we send our names, addresses and 25¢ to the University of Minnesota Pen Pal Club to be matched with prospective pen pals. I've always been interested in my Swedish heritage, so I asked for a pen pal from Sweden.

FRIENDS 30 YEARS and counting, are Kerstin (left, both photos) and Linda. The 1973 picture at top was taken on Linda's first of three trips to Sweden. Kerstin visited the U.S. as often.

A short time later, I received the name of a young lady my age. In the 30 years since, Kerstin and I have exchanged hundreds of letters and phone calls, and I've come to think of her as my "Swedish sister".

She's come to Iowa three times, and I've visited Sweden three times, including a trip with my parents for her wedding in 1982. That was quite an adventure—Kerstin and her new husband gave us a tour of Sweden from the northern Midnight Sun to the southern regions where my ancestors came from. How many newlyweds take their "family" along on their honeymoon?

My Swedish sister and I recently celebrated our 30th anniversary of international friendship. What a wonderful decision it was to invest that quarter!

Baby's Name Change Seemed Providential 6 Years Later

By April Clark, Archer, Florida

A DECISION my parents made when I was born may have seemed inconsequential at the time, but they certainly appreciated it 6 years later.

Throughout my mother's pregnancy, my dad and mom planned to name me Angela. Her due date was in March, but I held out for a couple of weeks and was born in April. On a whim, my parents named me for my birth month.

It was a good thing, too. Six years later, we adopted my little sister, then 3 years old—and her name was Angela!

It would've been mighty confusing for everyone to have two Angelas running around our house.

NO CONFUSION HERE. April (left) and Angela wore identical sleepers and slippers in 1973, but there was no doubt about which sister was which.

Big Decision Made Her 'Mom' to Seven Children

By Dorothy Stoner, Lockport, New York

WHEN I was 27, in 1957, I was working for the Department of the Army in Virginia and sharing a home with another government worker, a 54-year-old woman. It was a very quiet life, and each night I prayed that God would send somebody into my life so that I could be of use to someone. Little did I know my prayers would be answered...and then some.

One evening, my house mate brought home a 28-year-old man who had just become a second lieutenant. She introduced us, and we began to date. He was a single parent with six children.

We didn't marry until June 1961. It was a big decision, but I believed it was the answer to my prayers. In 1964, George and I had a son together. In 4 years, I'd gone from a single woman to the mother of seven!

Marrying George and becoming a mother to his children was the biggest decision I ever made, and I'll never regret it. It's been a very rewarding life.

Reluctant Quilter Made That Art Her Life's Work

By Suzanne Connor
Northfield,
New Hampshire

DOUBLE WEDDING. Sisters Yvonne (left) and Dora shared marriage ceremony in 1925.

MY GRANDMOTHER Yvonne and her sister were accomplished seamstresses and often made clothes for our family.

"Memere" taught me to sew at age 9, and we spent many happy hours together with needle and thread. She instilled a love of handwork that stayed with me into adulthood.

When I was 25, Aunt Dora wanted to teach me quilting, an art she and Memere had learned from their mother.

I wasn't particularly interested, but I was very fond of Aunt Dora, so I agreed. As it turned out, I loved quilting so much that I've made it my life's work.

By the time my son was born in 1983, I was receiving requests for hand-quilted pieces. Quilting enabled me to supplement our income while I stayed home with our child.

Since then, I've sold quilts at many juried shows throughout New England and have pieces on five of the seven continents.

People are always sur-

QUILT MAKER. Suzanne decided to follow Aunt Dora's lead and found her life's work.

prised that only one quilt hangs in my home—a velvet Victorian crazy quilt made by my great-grandmother. It is a treasure, as were all of the women it represents to me.

Memere and Aunt Dora are gone now, but I'm sure they're together, sewing for the smallest angels in heaven. I'm so grateful they took the time to pass a bit of their talent on to me.

Prayer for Guidance Made Them 'Northwest Pioneers'

By Shirley Van Mechelen, Everett, Washington

AFTER my husband's discharge from the Navy, we sat down to talk about our future. We both dreamed of farming, so Bill enrolled in animal husbandry classes at the university in Pullman, Washington. We put our house up for sale and prepared to move on campus with our baby girl.

But as we were packing, something didn't seem right. I told Bill I felt led to pray about our decision and ask God to

PIONEER SPIRIT filled Shirley and Bill when they moved to this wilderness home in Tyee, Washington in 1946. They delightfully added a baby son to their family.

open another door if He had other plans for us.

The next day, we had a surprise visit from an uncle Bill hadn't seen since childhood. Uncle Bern was starting a peeler mill on the Olympic Peninsula and wanted Bill to work for him. We took this as an answer to my prayer.

Our house sold the next week, and we scrambled to find another near the mill. God led us to a little house with wood heat, an old oil cookstove, no electricity and water piped from a spring behind the house. The pioneer spirit gripped us. We were elated!

Our 3 years there were among the happiest in 50-plus years of married life. We were surrounded by the beauty of nature and spent every spare minute fishing, hunting and exploring logging roads. God does answer prayer! And we did own two farms later on, so that mutual dream was fulfilled as well.

She Reached out in Friendship...
And Found a Daughter

By Mirja Bishop, Los Angeles, California

DEBBIE AND I met through our work as public health nurses. Our friendship began in March 1988, when I learned her mother was terminally ill.

I'd just lost my mother 2 months earlier, so my heart went out to Debbie. In the next few months, I called her periodically to share her sorrow and offer whatever support I could.

Debbie was now alone in the world. Her dad had died years earlier, and her only sibling's whereabouts were unknown. I was feeling alone, too, with no husband, no children and no siblings.

Debbie and I continued to share all our joys and sorrows. She supported me through the illness and death of my father. I was thrilled when she met and fell in love with Michael, who soon became her husband. I'd never been a mother, but now I felt like one.

Mother's Day 1989 was painful for both of us. We'd both lost our mothers and neither of us had chil-

DAUGHTER Debbie (left) and Mom Mirja have a new reason to celebrate Mother's Day each year.

dren, so there was nothing to celebrate. But we decided to get together anyway. We met for brunch and reminisced about our moms. It became an annual tradition.

In 1993, I began to think about adopting Debbie and decided to discuss it with her during our Mother's Day brunch. I don't know why it seemed so important, I just had to pursue it.

When Mother's Day came, I felt nervous because I'd rehearsed my little speech for days. I told her that I'd be honored if she'd allow me to adopt her. My dream was to be able to be and do all the things her mother would have. I felt as if Debbie's mom was directing me in some spiritual way, and that this was my destiny.

Made Things Final

Debbie was pleased with the idea. We consulted a lawyer, and in October 1993, we appeared in Children's Court to finalize the adoption. I was 56; Debbie was 36 years old and 3 months pregnant.

Being a mother didn't come as naturally as I'd expected, but Debbie and I have learned how to be mother and daughter. We share our lives, we support each other, and we love each other. We are a family. Today, I not only have a lovely daughter, but a gorgeous grandson.

When I tell people about the adoption, the first reaction is usually, "Why would you do that?" I can't really answer that, except to say that it felt so right and wonderful. And I really believe that our mothers in heaven are smiling down on us as they share their memories.

This Quick Decision Taught Educators Some Lessons

By Sandra Taylor, Indiana, Pennsylvania

A HASTY DECISION made by my husband and me paid off in a rewarding career for him, college degrees for our children and an unforgettable adventure for me.

It began in 1938, when Alvin and I had been married 4 years. We were living in Bedford County, Pennsylvania, where Alvin taught in a one-room school.

Though he represented the fourth generation in his family to teach in that county, Alvin was miserable in his job. One evening in March, his cousin Evelyn and her husband Bus dropped by. They had good news.

Evelyn worked at the Mother's Assistance Office in Indiana County, and she'd heard of an opening for a caseworker. She inquired about the position and found Alvin's education qualified him. There was one catch...he'd have to start the next morning!

Alvin was stuck. He'd signed a contract to teach the whole school year. But if he wanted the new job, he had to leave with Bus and Evelyn immediately!

We decided he had to do it. Meanwhile, *I* would teach Alvin's pupils for the rest of the year.

Could She Do That?

With all the confidence of youth, I was sure I could handle the job. I'd earned my teaching certificate before we'd married, but had never gone beyond student teaching.

We woke our baby, Pauline, tore down her crib and left our home in the middle of the night. Alvin dropped us off at his mother's farm and departed with Evelyn and Bus.

I'd never set foot in a one-room school much less teach in one, but on Thursday morning I packed a lunch of six crackers and a pint of tomato juice and set off on snow-covered roads in our '34 Plymouth coupe.

I left early to start a fire for the children—some of them walked 3 miles to get to school.

At 4 feet 5 inches tall, I wasn't sure if I could control those tall strong farm boys in seventh and eighth grades. But my answer was waiting when I arrived at school.

Young Bill Mowry was a 6-foot-tall student who immediately adopted me. He took over the fire-making chores, and if any older boys misbehaved, he just stood up, and the trouble-maker backed down.

As the days passed, the school board members heard rumors that the Pleasant Hollow

MADE THE GRADES. Sandra (front) instilled importance of education in (from left) Wilson, Pauline, John, Barbara and Joe.

School had a new teacher. I hadn't even considered contacting them to explain. Alvin was gone, it was too late for them to find another teacher, and it was unlikely they'd fire me and face an unfinished school year.

One morning after I'd started class, a man showed up at our door. He stood there observing, and I taught as if he was not there. The school board member left at recess time, apparently satisfied at the job I was doing.

Proved She Was Qualified

Soon I received a letter from the superintendent demanding I send proof of my certification. I did…and received it back without an accompanying letter.

The students and I finished our year happily, and I promised to let them out of school one day early if they did well on their exams. They did gratifyingly well.

My job was finished, so I packed up Pauline and left to join Alvin in Indiana County.

We'd lived there before, having both graduated from Indiana State Teacher's College (now Indiana University of Pennsylvania). It had been our dream to send our children to our alma mater. Evelyn made that dream come true with the hasty-yet-wise decision she encouraged us to make in 1938.

Alvin spent the rest of his working days in the rewarding career of social work with the poor and elderly. And all five of our children eventually earned degrees at Indiana University.

This 'Loan Decision' Changed A Life Forever

By Patricia Kile, Greentown, Pennsylvania

THE DECISION that changed my life was made for me in 1941, when I was 7. I was the middle child of seven, growing up on a farm in northeastern Pennsylvania.

The three older boys helped with the milking and outside

SOON TO LEAVE the family was 7-year-old Patricia, in 1941. She's the tallest girl, wearing a patterned dress.

chores, and we girls helped Mom in the house.

Mother was swamped trying to cook for seven children and a hired man, gardening, canning, doing laundry with a wringer washer, keeping the wood and coal fires going, emptying ashes and feeding the chickens.

Even on Sundays she seldom rested. Occasionally on Sundays, Aunt Leona and Uncle Lou would come to visit, and I enjoyed them.

Aunt Leona was a teacher and loved kids, so she seemed very special to me when she talked with me or read stories. Uncle Lou was a dentist and quite wealthy (at least from our perspective on the farm). Little did I know what an important role this couple would come to play in my life.

Aunt Leona was unable to have children, and she and Uncle Lou desperately wanted them. They approached my parents about "loaning" one of us to them. "You can take one of the girls—they're useless," my father said. "But you can't have the boys. I need them on the farm."

New Life Lay Ahead

After a trial weekend visit, I was sent to live with Aunt Leona and Uncle Lou. My meager supply of clothing was packed in a paper bag, and off I went to live an entirely new life.

My aunt and uncle's home was only 50 miles away, but life there was so different! I was now a pampered, loved "only child". I had my own bedroom with new furniture, took trips and vacations and had my aunt's undivided attention.

During World War II, I helped Aunt Leona with her airplane-spotting duties. We made many crafts, some of which I still cherish. On our long daily walks, she taught me to be aware of the different trees and plants, and she helped me collect insects in the woods.

Uncle Lou spent time with me, too. I often sat with him in his lab while he made plates and bridges. We listened to *The Lone Ranger* and *Inner Sanctum* on the radio, and he taught me how to develop X-rays in the basement. Sometimes we'd go to the lake, where he taught me how to row a boat and fish.

TODAY, Patricia has happy memories of Mom's wise decision.

I visited my family every month or so, but began to feel more like a city cousin than a sister.

Off to College

After graduating from high school, I went to the college of my choice and majored in elementary education—just like Aunt Leona. When I got married, my aunt and uncle planned the wedding, and Uncle Lou gave me away. Mom came to the wedding, but my father didn't. He still thought girls were "worthless".

But I never felt worthless. Between the selfless desire of my Mom for me to have the best, and my aunt's devotion and dedication to me, I became a productive member of society.

Shortly before my mom died, I made a comment about her "giving me away". Hurt by this careless remark, she said gently, "I didn't give you away. I loaned you out for your own good." And it was.

I'll never know how different my life would have been if I'd stayed on the farm. But I wouldn't have gone to the same high school and certainly not to college, where I met my husband.

One of my sisters recently admitted that the rest of my siblings felt sorry for me because Aunt Leona seemed so strict. I'd always felt like the lucky one!

Chapter Five

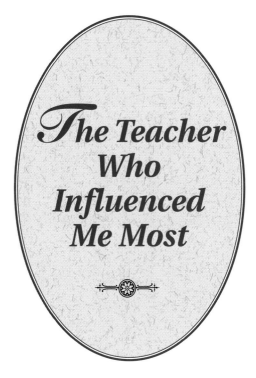

The Teacher
Who
Influenced
Me Most

Teacher Became Mentor
And Lifelong Friend

By Jo Ann Peak, Colorado Springs, Colorado

IN 1945, I was starting seventh grade in the little coal mining town of West Frankfort, Illinois. Margie B. Lilley came into my life that year, and I doubt I'd have taught school for 36 years if it hadn't been for her positive influence.

"Margie B" taught handwriting and spelling, and she had a reputation as a stern but fair disciplinarian. She taught strict Palmer Method penmanship, and no one was permitted to change a single letter or hold a pen incorrectly.

I never admired anyone as much as Margie B, and I tried to do everything just as she instructed. She seemed to bring out the best in me.

One day, she said I was one of the best penmanship students in junior high. Would I like to do a special job for her every Friday after school? My heart almost leaped out of my chest. I didn't even know what the job was, but I wanted to hug her.

My task was to write a different quotation in colored chalk on all the classroom blackboards. Margie B had been doing it herself, but thought I could do it as well as she did.

Took Pride in Penmanship

For the rest of that school year and all of eighth grade, my penmanship appeared in every classroom. I was proud to be entrusted with such a task, and it made me try to perfect my handwriting even more.

When I started high school, I continued to visit Margie B after school. By now we were good friends, and I could share my private thoughts with her.

The summer after graduation, Margie B offered to help me get my Palmer Method supervisor's certificates. I started college that fall, coming home on weekends to work in my father's bakery. Then I went to Margie B's for penmanship lessons. Before my freshman year ended, I had my supervisor's certificates.

I received my B.S. in education in 3-1/2 years, and it

was Margie B's encouragement that got me through. My parents were immigrants from Macedonia, and Dad didn't think it was important for a girl to have an education. Without Margie B's influence and help, I probably would have ended up working in Dad's bakery. She was my model and mentor.

I took a teaching job in West Frankfort, but soon moved away with my husband, who was in the Air Force. Margie B and I became even closer as we corresponded for the next 25 years. Whenever I came home for a visit, I was just as eager to see my dear friend as my own relatives.

Her Firmness and Fairness Followed

In 36 years of teaching, nothing I learned from Margie B was wasted. Her firmness and fairness remained uppermost in my mind, and I always found ways to relate spelling and handwriting skills to any subject.

Though Margie B is not around for me to talk with anymore, her handwriting is tucked away throughout my home. Whenever I open a scrapbook, I find a report card, diploma or certificate with her writing on it. As long as I live, a part of her will always be part of me. Margie B. Lilley was my mentor, my inspiration and my idol.

EIGHTH GRADE HOMEROOM class photo from 1948 includes teacher Margie B (far right) and Jo Ann Peak, seated third from right in center row.

Naive Farm Girl Found Confidence to Succeed

By Carol Battaglia
Land O' Lakes, Florida

SUCCESS! Thanks to her teacher, Carol Battaglia did graduate from high school and made this dress for the occasion in 1950.

MOTHER DIED when I was in first grade, and 8 years later, during the 1940s, Dad sold our northern Wisconsin farm and moved us south to Racine County. There, I'd attend a city school for the first time.

Each morning before school, I milked two cows by hand, fed the chickens, did other chores, then quickly washed up and changed clothes. I ate breakfast on the run.

Going to a city school turned out to be devastating for a naive farm girl. I couldn't make friends. No one wanted to talk with me or eat lunch with me. Little did I know that I smelled like a cow because I hadn't washed my hair after milking. All the farm girls I knew washed their hair on Saturdays.

After a while, I gave up. I'd always done well at my old one-room country school, and now I was failing. I never heard a word the teachers said.

One day, my homeroom teacher, Mrs. Bolten, asked me to stay after school. She said she knew I could learn, but didn't think I was listening. I was beyond tears or feeling. We sat there, eye to eye, for what seemed like forever.

Finally, Mrs. Bolten said, "You're a smart little girl. Every night you're going to stay after school, and I'm going to help you pass. Every morning after chores, you wash your hair, even if it's wet when you get here. You're going all the way through high school."

And I did. I had lots of friends and excellent grades—all because one tough lady took the trouble to guide me through a difficult time.

Support Turned Potential Dropout into Star Pupil

By Nancy Schave, Skagway, Alaska

IN THE LATE 1950s, I was in seventh grade, making D's and F's. Two older siblings had already dropped out, and I was in school only about half the time.

One day, Mrs. Ilah Page took me into the teachers' lounge, a sacred place that students never entered. Her message was simple: "I know you're smart. I care about you. Why aren't you in school?"

I said I didn't get breakfast (although that was my own choice) and made other excuses. What I said wasn't important. What *was* important was that Mrs. Page took the time to encourage me. She even brought me sandwiches each morning and sent me to the cafeteria to eat them.

I never missed another day of school and graduated with honors. I worked my way through college, using every loan and scholarship available to me, and finished my first degree in 3 years. Later, I received my doctorate and worked as a teacher, counselor, principal, and finally, a school superintendent.

No one who knew me at age 13 ever would have said, "There goes someone who could become an educational leader." No one, that is, except Mrs. Page.

Though Small in Stature, He Stood Tall in Classroom

By Carl Crumpton, Topeka, Kansas

I WAS always the smallest boy in my class at Ogden (Kansas) Grade School during the 1930s. Bigger boys bullied me at recess, and I was no match for them. I just didn't have the size, weight or strength to compete on the playground.

EXCELLENCE in academics helped Carl Crumpton become bigger in the eyes of his peers. "I'm the little guy with the big ears at the right arm of the principal," notes Carl.

But in fifth and sixth grades, Miss Alice Garvin showed me that I *could* hold my own in the classroom. With her encouragement, I began to excel in reading, writing and arithmetic. "Miss Alice" measured her students from the neck up. By that standard, I was as big as any of my classmates.

As my study and hard work began to pay off, the other students showed me a new respect. By the time I graduated from eighth grade, no one was bullying me anymore. I was still the smallest in size, but I was large in self-respect.

I thank Miss Alice for taking a different measure of her students. She boosted my self-esteem and helped me to recognize my strengths. Without her, I might have blindly continued trying to compete on the wrong playing field. She redirected me down the right path when I reached a fork in the road.

As for the bullies, I guess they helped me, too. During World War II, I didn't think Marine Corps DI's were all that bad—not after I'd been toughened up by the bullying of those Ogden Grade School kids.

Punishment Put Prankster
On the Straight and Narrow

By Robert DeBuhr, Rainier, Oregon

WHEN I FAILED to take education seriously, Miss Roberts got to the seat of the problem.

She made the mistake of letting us fifth-graders know she was deathly afraid of frogs and snakes. One morning, my buddy and I arrived early and deposited a small garter snake and one very lively frog in her middle desk drawer. Then we took our seats and waited in excited anticipation. We didn't have long to wait.

When Miss Roberts opened the drawer for a piece of chalk, the frog and snake saw an opportunity to escape. Poor Miss Roberts screamed, threw her arms into the air and jumped back into the blackboard.

The class roared. She quickly recovered her composure and pointed right at us. Somehow she knew just who the culprits were.

She marched us into the hall and spanked us, saying, "This hurts me more than it does you." That was debatable. Then she took us to the principal's office. We would have to bring our mothers to school the next morning to be reenrolled.

When my father got home that night and heard what had happened, I got another licking, along with some advice about the benefits of education versus horseplay. I'm sure Miss Roberts straightened me out for life the day she bent me over her lap.

Teacher's Friendship
Lasted a Lifetime

By Otto Harris, Taylors, South Carolina

I FIRST MET Mrs. Annie P. Cunningham in 1930, when I was in second grade at Westville Grammar High School in Greenville, South Carolina. I happened to be fighting with another boy at the time.

Mrs. Cunningham, a high school teacher, was patrolling the playground during recess. She jerked me up by the collar and sent us both to the principal's office for a whipping.

After that, Mrs. Cunningham took an interest in me, even though I was a long way from becoming one of her students.

NO-NONSENSE teacher, Annie Cunningham, appears at center rear in this 1939 photo. Author Otto Harris is the second from left.

As the grammar school years passed, she always encouraged me to study and get good grades.

On my first day as an eighth-grader, all of us were talking and laughing. Suddenly we heard what sounded like three pistol shots. We looked up and there she stood, snapping her fingers.

"When you hear me snap my fingers, it means to be quiet.

I am Mrs. Annie P. Cunningham, your literature teacher. You children are here to learn, and I will do my best to teach you."

Then she laid out her rules: "Number 1, there will be no excuses for not getting your homework done. Number 2, you will be polite at all times. Number 3, I will require you to read every article in the *Reader's Digest* each month, and one other book, and make a book report on it. Number 4, there will be no complaining. Does everyone understand?"

All Students Obeyed

We all said, "Yes, Mrs. Cunningham." Just her presence commanded respect.

Then Mrs. Cunningham said, "Let us pray." She prayed for wisdom and patience, so she could help us learn, and asked the Lord's blessings and guidance for each student.

Mrs. Cunningham taught me English and literature for 4 years. In all that time, I never heard her raise her voice or scold a pupil. Just the look in her eyes was enough to set anyone straight. If a student was having trouble in class, she was always willing to help during recess or after school.

Thanks to Mrs. Cunningham, I graduated with honors. I joined the Navy, and we corresponded often. When war broke out and I was captured by the Japanese, she prayed before every class for my safe return.

After 40 months as a POW, I came home. When Mrs. Cunningham heard the news, she walked out on her class to come see me.

I remained in the Navy, but visited Mrs. Cunningham whenever I came home. When I had a family of my own, my wife and children came along. My wife had been one of her pupils, too.

After I retired, I was able to visit Mrs. Cunningham more often. Eventually she was put in a nursing home. I visited her every day for 2 years, until an illness in my own family forced

LIFELONG FRIEND of author, Mrs. Cunningham holds his grandkids.

me to cut back those visits to one or two per week.

Mrs. Cunningham told everybody I was the son she never had. She loved to reminisce about her school days and referred to all her former students as "her children". In 48 years of teaching, she shaped the lives of thousands.

Mrs. Cunningham has passed on now, but I often think back on the good times we shared. She was more than a teacher. She was a counselor, confidante and a true friend, and I'm a better person for having known her.

Nudge Toward Scholarship Led to Engineering Career

By Erwin Branahl, Ferguson, Missouri

MY GRADES at Zion Lutheran School in St. Louis, Missouri were only slightly above average, but my parents accepted that. After all, I got A's in conduct and effort.

Shortly before graduation, a former teacher of mine called my parents in for a conference. Each year, the public high school awarded a 4-year university scholarship to our school's top-ranking student. Mr. Grundemann assured my parents I could win it, if they could motivate me. Until then, college had been out of reach because of the Great Depression.

Mr. Grundemann's confidence in me was all I needed to focus on winning the scholarship—and I did. I obtained an engineering degree, received a Navy commission and was sent to radar school.

The Navy sent me to Bowdoin College and the Massachusetts Institute of Technology, where I trained to work on a radar system to be used in the invasion of Japan.

When the war ended, I had the equivalent of a master's degree from one of the leading engineering schools in the country.

I enjoyed a 41-year career with McDonnell-Douglas, ending as an executive vice president. It all was made possible because Mr. Grundemann recognized my ability and was interested enough to encourage me to use it.

I don't even want to consider what my life would have been like if I'd continued to slide through the easy way.

Teacher's Help Smoothed Transition to Bigger School

By Joelyn Smith, Buena Vista, Colorado

I GREW UP on a mountainous cattle ranch Dad had homesteaded in 1920 near Golden, Colorado. Because of the severe winters, our one-room school was in session from March to November. Our teacher scheduled frequent field trips in summer, with picnics, hiking, a little geology and lots of nature study.

All this was possible because Mrs. Ramstetter enjoyed teaching so much—and because Mountain House School never had more than 5 or 6 students.

At 13, I moved on to a high school with more than 100 students. I was having a tough time adjusting to such a big school, and when Dad died unexpectedly, I refused to go back.

Mrs. Ramstetter was recertified to teach high school courses just so I could finish ninth grade at Mountain House. I graduated from Golden High School 3 years later with a scholarship to a business school.

Years later, when my own kids started school, I realized how

THE ENTIRE STUDENT BODY did the maypole dance at Mountain House School in 1937. Joelyn Smith, 10, is at right.

fortunate I had been to have Mrs. Ramstetter in my life. I only wish I'd taken the time to tell her what a special lady she was.

She has passed on, and I'll probably always feel guilty for not thanking her in person, but I know she's a teaching angel in heaven. Thank you Alice Ramstetter. I love you!

After 40 Years, He Still Draws on Coach's Inspiration

By David Williams
Newbury Park, California

FEATHER MERCHANT? Not here! David Williams learned a lot about himself on this practice field, thanks to Kinger.

BOB KING—"Kinger", as everyone called him—was the teacher who most influenced my life. He was my teacher, my coach and my friend.

I got to know Kinger in the 1950s when I played varsity football at Shortridge High School in Indianapolis, Indiana. He was a legend—a tough taskmaster on the field, but a guy with a great sense of humor.

At practices, Kinger guided us through a tough half-hour workout. The killer was lying flat on our backs in full uniform, then lifting our legs 6 inches. Kinger would yell out, "Up 6 inches...hold 'em...hold 'em... down!"

This went on and on until we were all moaning and groaning.

Rumor had it that if you let your legs down before Kinger gave the command, he'd jump up and down on your stomach. We held 'em and waited.

At the end of each practice, we ran wind sprints across the field, with Kinger yelling, "Get up in there! Don't be last!" If you were last, you were a feather merchant. To this day, I don't know what a feather merchant is, but I still don't want to be one.

On the field, Kinger gave advice and guidance without embarrassing anyone. He'd just walk a player away from the others for a private conversation. He never put us down in front of our peers, and we respected him for that.

LEGENDARY teacher and coach, Bob King, was named Man of the Year by the class of 1957, Shortridge High.

Kinger was the team's scout, so he didn't see us play on Friday nights. The one game he got to watch was the last of the year, against our arch-rivals. I was suiting up for that game my senior year when I found a note from Kinger in my locker.

It said I was about to play the best game of my life. In fact, I would play so well that I'd surprise myself. I put the note inside my helmet. Kinger proved to be right.

Kinger knew the art of listening, and he didn't preach. He never gave up on us. Kinger was the only teacher I ever had who gave his home phone number to the kids. We all knew we could talk to him if we needed advice or got into a jam.

Kinger's name always comes up at our reunions, along with new stories made safe to tell by the passage of time. It's amazing how many of us turned to Kinger for advice.

I never saw Kinger again after graduation in 1957. After college, I became a teacher—and an assistant football coach. Now I was the one yelling, "Get up in there! Don't be last!" and "Up 6 inches!"

I've never regretted becoming a teacher or copying Kinger's methods. I go running every day to stay in shape, and I hate it.

My course has a hill, and when I reach it in the early-morning hours with no one else around, I speak for my ears only. "Get up in there, Williams! Don't be last! You don't want to be a feather merchant, do you?"

Teacher's Encouragement Sparked Writing Career

By Viola Zumault
Kansas City, Missouri

FROM THE TIME I was old enough to read, I had a love affair with poetry. In grade school, I wrote rhymed verse. By high school, I had sold a few poems and articles to magazines.

My high school English teacher, Miss Lena Boley, encouraged me to pursue a career in writing, but my parents weren't enthusiastic. Writers were considered strange, or loners, and only a few poets were able to make a decent living. They insisted I prepare for a teaching career. I did so, but I never lost my desire to write.

On graduation night, my beloved teacher took me aside and said, "Viola, promise me that you will never stop writing poetry. God has given you a rare talent, and you owe it to

PRETTY POETESS Viola Zumault, in a photo taken on her 16th birthday, May 7, 1921.

Him to use it. Someday you will have your own book of poetry, and I will be the first to rejoice with you."

At that moment, my goal was set. I solemnly vowed to

write that book, not for myself, but for that wonderful person who believed in me.

I went to college, taught school, married and had a 37-year-long career in real estate, but I never forgot my promise. All through those busy years, Miss Boley kept in touch, cheering from the sidelines.

When my first book came off the press, it was addressed to the person who had inspired and encouraged me, and to whom I give all the credit for a successful writing career. I've had over 1,000 poems and two books of poetry published, thanks to one dedicated caring teacher who inspired a little country girl to never stop writing.

Girls in Integrated School Learned to Respect Each Other

By Ann De Lacy, Olney, Maryland

WISE TEACHER Ola Hendren helped students of many races accept others.

ON A beautiful summer day in 1965, Jonesville High School in North Carolina was integrated for the first time. I was one of the first African-American students—a nervous 15-year-old. But as the oldest child, I knew it was important that I represent my family well.

I had the luck of being placed in Mrs. Ola Hendren's home economics class, though I don't remember signing up for it. I always fancied myself too smart for cooking and sewing.

Mrs. Hendren was kind, fair, smart and had wonderful classroom control. Through her, we girls of different races learned a mutual respect for each other. She taught us to appreciate the things we had in common and celebrate our differences. She exposed us to new ideas, too. Imagine, *learning* something in a home economics class!

TODAY, Ann De Lacy follows her favorite teacher's lead, teaching home economics.

When I graduated, I went to on to college—and became a home economics teacher! Today, we call it "family and consumer science".

After 24 years of teaching, I still use many of the concepts I learned from Mrs. Hendren. Of all the courses I've taken over the years, Mrs. Hendren's have had the greatest impact on my life.

Chronic Procrastinator Found Ways to Keep Up

By Helena Heider, Billings, Montana

"DR. ABBOTT, may I be excused from class to attend a funeral?"

"Of course. Just hand in your written assignment."

"It isn't ready." My college assignments were rarely handed in on time. I worked hard, but couldn't meet the deadlines.

Dr. Abbott said, "When Gabriel blows his horn, you'll be way out there, shouting, 'Wait for me! Wait for me!'"

That hit home. I began to zero in on what came first. What could I delay? What could I eliminate?

Now, I pay my bills when I get them. I send gifts and cards early. I shop at sales as soon as they start. I do outside chores first to take advantage of good weather, winterize early and prepare for as much of the future as I can see.

Meet you at the gate, Dr. Abbott!

Admiring Student Followed Shop Teacher's Footsteps

By Carlington Kuglin, Modesto, California

THE TEACHER who changed my life was Walter Leroy Stephenson, but everybody called him "Steve". He was my shop teacher from junior high through high school in Columbia City, Indiana. We worked with wood and did advanced drafting.

After graduating from high school in 1939, I served in the Air Force, got married and decided to study architecture. I applied at a university in Cincinnati, Ohio, but it was wartime, and since I wasn't an Ohio resident, I was refused.

On the way home, I stopped to visit Steve, then living in Yorktown, Indiana. When I told Steve my problem, he said, "Do you remember all those times I asked you to take charge of my shop class? I often watched you from outside the classroom, and you always did a tremendous job. Why don't you go to school here at Ball State and become a shop teacher?"

SHOP TALK. Carlington Kuglin (above) will never forget "Steve" (inset, 1939 photo).

I did go to Ball State University in Muncie and visited Steve often in nearby Yorktown. I graduated in 3 years and got a teaching job in California. Whenever I came back to Indiana, I always visited Steve. I named my first son after him.

Years later, my mother wrote that the Yorktown church was having a "this is your life" program for Steve. He had taught there for a few years and made a big impression on the community.

I flew back that weekend for the program. I was proud to honor the man who had inspired me to become a teacher and who had been a friend to so many young children.

One Teacher Saved His Life; Another Shaped His Career

By Bruce Holmes, Macomb, Illinois

ON March 30, 1938, a terrible thunderstorm struck outside the schoolhouse in Columbus, Kansas. Our fifth-grade teacher, Loren Wellman, calmly told us to move out into the hall. I had ducked under my desk in fright and was the last student to reach the door.

As I passed through the door, a brick fell on my head. A tornado had just ripped off the roof above us, along with the two outer walls of our classroom and most of our bolted-down desks. I had escaped death by seconds.

CLOSE CALL! Alert teachers moved students to interior halls just before a tornado blew off the roof and some outer walls of this school. Miraculously, no one was seriously hurt.

If Mr. Wellman hadn't ordered us into the hall when he did, *all* of us would have died. The tornado killed several people in town, but there were no serious injuries at the school.

A year later, I saw more of Mr. Wellman's leadership when I joined his Boy Scout troop. He impressed me with the importance of the Scout Oath and Scout Law. They were major factors in molding my character, and I still try to follow those guidelines today.

Another teacher, Dell Davidson, led the Scouts on bird hikes. I found birds so fascinating that Mr. Davidson continued taking me on hikes after I finished my Scout requirement. I became something of a local bird expert, which helped build my self-confidence.

I will be forever grateful that this gentleman spent so much of his spare time helping one small boy. I'm not sure I would have done the same if I'd been in his place.

My interest in birds led me to the broader field of biology. I eventually earned a Ph.D. in that subject and taught college biology for 41 years.

Other than my father, Mr. Wellman and Mr. Davidson were the men who most influenced my life. One saved my life and helped mold my character, and the other determined my career. They are my heroes.

Teacher Opened Door To Girl's College Education

By Venus Bardanouve, Harlem, Montana

MISS LUCILLE McVey was not my teacher. I never took one of her classes. And yet she changed my life.

It was 1935, and I would graduate from high school in St. Paul, Nebraska in a few weeks. Although I was a good student, there was no thought of further education. The Depression had put jobs, money and opportunity out of most graduates' reach. I was grateful when the local telephone company offered me a job.

One day, Miss McVey stopped me in the hall for a talk. "Venus, you ought to go to college," she said. "My family lives in Lincoln, where there are several colleges and universities. I'm there in summer, and if I can help you in any way, I'll do it."

I worked for a year after graduation, living at home and saving every penny. Then I wrote to Miss McVey. She introduced me to a doctor's family in Lincoln, where I worked in exchange for room and board while attending Nebraska Wesleyan University. I went on to get my degree and become a speech pathologist.

DOCTORAL GRADUATE Venus and her husband, Francis, both received doctorates in letters from Montana State University, 1996. "Miss McVey's influence reached a long way!" Venus says.

No one in my family had ever earned a college degree, and I wouldn't have known the first steps to take toward one without Miss McVey's help. I'll always be grateful to her. She changed my life—and the lives of all my family to come.

College Instructor Found Child's Wisdom Worth Sharing

By Robert Dockery, Morganton, North Carolina

THE TEACHER who changed my life was only 6 years old!

I teach horticulture at Western Piedmont Community College in Morganton. One day, a student in my plant identification class was unable to get a baby-sitter, so she brought her little girl along. This happens, and all we could do was make the best of it. The child walked around campus with us as we identified and talked about various trees.

After around 2 hours, I felt a tug on my pants leg. The little girl was trying to get my attention.

DR. BOB at work in outdoor classroom. The photograph was taken by the mother of the 6-year-old recalled in this story.

When I looked down, she looked up and said, "Doctor Bob, what is more 'portant—is it the funny names we call the trees, or to 'preciate their being here?"

We were all struck by the clarity of this child's view of the world. From that day to this, I share this story with my plant identification classes on the first day and remind them to take time to "'preciate" the trees.

That little girl is now a grown woman with children of her own. But I still see her young face, feel her tugging on my pants leg, and a warm feeling comes over me as I retell the story of her wisdom.

Chapter Six

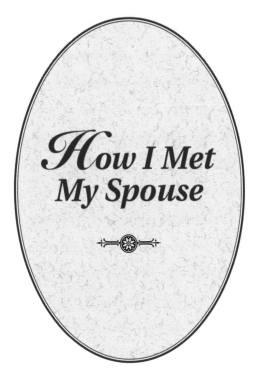

How I Met My Spouse

She Couldn't Wait For Chance to Serve Cute GI

By Dortha Wood
Burlington, Iowa

GI PHIL as he appeared before meeting Dortha. Photo was taken near Reims, Germany in 1945.

IN FEBRUARY 1946, I was 15 years old and working as a waitress. One day, a young man with dark wavy hair came into the cafe, parked his duffel bag, played the jukebox, ordered some coffee and asked me to call him a cab. He'd just been discharged from the Army.

When he left, I told the other waitress, "Boy, he was cute!" I pleaded with her to let me wait on him if he ever came in again.

The next day, I was breading tenderloins in the kitchen, my hands a mess, when I heard the other waitress yell, "Dortha, you got a customer!" She left my cute young man sitting perplexed at the counter.

After I washed my hands and sheepishly went out to take his order, he asked, "Didn't she want to wait on me?" I said, "No, but I did."

I've been waiting on him ever since. After 50 years of marriage, I'm still thankful for the waitress who wouldn't wait on my cute young man.

A HAPPY WIFE and mother was Dortha Wood after meeting Phil. Dortha posed for this photo in 1952.

2 Weeks of Making Change Finally Got Her Attention

By Vyvyan Gardner, Canyon City, Oregon

DURING college break in the summer of 1947, I was hired as the receptionist for a fruit-packing plant. The office manager admonished me that the "office girls" were not to fraternize with the boys who worked in the plant. My desk was right in front of her office, so I took that advice, until...

One young man began coming to my desk several times a day to get change for the nickel Coke machine. I gave him plenty of nickels, but kept our conversations short.

After about 2 weeks of this, I gave him a half-dollar, a quarter, two dimes and *one* nickel. "Now you'll have to come back," I said.

Our first date followed. We got engaged on the third date and married 6 months later.

Today, my husband jokes that no one else in the plant ever had to get change from the office, because he always had enough for everybody. He also wondered if I was slow in picking up on the reason for all those visits, until I gave him that single nickel.

CHANGE FOR THE BETTER. Fredrick and Vyvyan Gardner were married in 1948, with Donald Shores and Dorothy Morris attending.

Stranded Schoolteacher Met Husband-to-Be In Snowstorm

By Edell Swanson
Morris, Minnesota

I WAS TEACHING at a country school, commuting the 20 miles from home in my Model A Ford.

One day in January 1946, with 4 to 5 inches of fresh snow on the ground, a strong wind came up. Parents soon appeared to pick up their children.

As the last child left, a young Navy man named Douglas appeared from the farmhouse across the road. His parents didn't think I could get home and invited me to stay with them until the storm abated. The next morning, the family took me to

LET IT SNOW! Being snowbound didn't bother Douglas and Edell Swanson. They were married June, 1947.

town in a sled. My father met me and took me home.

In late May, Douglas again appeared at the school door and asked me for a date. He had just been discharged from the Navy. We were married a year later and now have eight children, 28 grandchildren and one great-grandchild.

If that snowstorm hadn't occurred during the 2 weeks Doug was home on leave, I doubt we would've started dating.

Airman Refused to Give Up
When His Date Ditched Him

By Judith Goleaner, Cahokia, Illinois

OUR most-requested family story is the one about how my parents met. None of us ever tire of hearing this family legend!

My father and his best friend were stationed at Scott Air Force Base near St. Louis, Missouri in 1946. Dad's friend was dating Mom's best friend, and they decided to arrange a blind date for my parents, much to Mom's dismay. She had no desire to go out with a strange airman.

Mom was dragged kicking and screaming to meet Dad. They met at a trolley car and decided to take it to the movies. As the car pulled away, Dad turned to speak to Mom, but she wasn't there. He turned to the window just in time to see her standing at the curb, smiling and waving good-bye.

Mom headed home, satisfied she had neatly avoided this dreaded blind date—only to find Dad there waiting for her! They were married 3 months later.

Colorful Carnation
Gave Him Green Light
To Ask for Date

By Arthur Eddy
Buffalo, New York

DURING the Depression, I delivered milk door-to-door for my uncle. When the routes were changed, I found myself delivering milk to the home of a lovely blonde girl.

The first time I collected at her

CONTENTED COUPLE. The Eddys were married in 1941, thanks to a carnation.

house, she answered the door, and we talked for a bit. A couple of mornings later, I found a green carnation in one of the empty milk bottles. I figured she'd put it there for me.

The next morning, I left a note, saying I'd come by the next night to take her to a show. I had no idea whether she would even go out with me, but when I got there, she was all set to go. That was 60 years ago.

That green carnation affected the lives of 11 people, seven of whom wouldn't be here today if I hadn't taken that fork in the road.

Empty Chair at Luncheon Changed Her Life Forever

By Frances Albright, Montevallo, Alabama

MY high school graduating class got together for a lunch every December. Several times I'd noticed a distinguished-looking white-haired man named Jack, but we never had much of an opportunity to talk.

At the 1994 luncheon, I was looking for a place to sit. The only empty chair was next to Jack, and he invited me to take it. Before long, neither

LIFE BEGAN AT 70 for Frances and Jack, who married in May, 1995.

of us knew what we were eating, or even where we were. We went to a hockey game on our first date.

Both of us were widowed and felt we were leading full lives, but changed our minds after we found each other. Before long, we realized we loved each other. We married in May 1995, and our children were delighted. Between us, we have seven children and 14 grandchildren.

We're extremely happy and fulfilled, and our love continues to grow. Life can begin at 70! What if I hadn't sat next to this wonderful man that December day? An empty chair changed my life forever.

Beautiful Penmanship Led to Letter-Perfect Romance

By Albert McAllister, Jackson, Mississippi

DURING my basic training in World War II, a buddy returned from Christmas leave and told me about a girl he'd met on the train. I didn't think much about it until some time later, when I saw an envelope on his bunk with the most beautiful handwriting I'd ever seen. I thought, "That's the handwriting of the girl I'm going to marry."

My buddy gave me Mary Ann's name and address, and we started writing in April 1942. Our correspondence continued for the next 3 years. We met after my discharge in November 1945 and married 2 months later.

When I worked up the nerve to tell Mary Ann I didn't have a high school diploma, she simply asked, "Would you like to have one?" With her help,

PEN FRIENDS Albert and Mary Ann married, earned degrees—and happiness.

I enrolled in a correspondence school and finished the 4-year program in 2 years.

Then Mary Ann asked if I wanted to earn a college degree. I enrolled at the University of Nebraska and earned a bachelor's degree in retailing. Mary Ann went, too, and earned a master's degree in counseling.

What would have happened if I hadn't seen that envelope? What would have happened if my wife hadn't helped me to get an education? Mary Ann changed my life forever.

Bold Move Turned Their Friendship Into Romance

By Anita Freed
Portage, Michigan

THE FIRST TIME I saw the young man who was to be my husband, my heart skipped a beat. It was the early 1930s, and he was crossing our driveway, entering my dad's office to apply for a job.

Bob and I were formally introduced several months later, on my 21st birthday. We became friends, though we didn't date. I was always wishing!

DOUBLE HITCHED. Because Anita hitched a ride with Bob, they spent 56 years hitched as husband and wife.

One evening, I was to meet another young man for a date after a dental appointment. But when I came out of the dentist's office, I saw Bob's car parked near the movie theater. I quickly forgot my date and jumped into Bob's car and waited.

When Bob came out of the theater, I asked him to take me

home. We took the long way around. It was the beginning of a beautiful relationship that lasted 56 years.

Bob and I had a wonderful life together. He was a good father to our three sons and a faithful loving husband. I'm alone now, but have a loving family and beautiful memories. The last words Bob spoke to me were of his love for me.

Teen Romeo Signaled His Juliet with an Owl Call

By Ruby Neese, Liberty, North Carolina

MY PARENTS were teenagers when they met, and they instantly fell in love. But they weren't allowed to see each other.

Mama's parents didn't like Daddy's family because he had an older brother who was always in trouble. Never mind that Daddy was a good boy—they judged the whole family by one bad apple.

No matter how much Mama begged, she was not allowed to see Daddy. She had no choice but to sneak out to see him.

Daddy would come to the woods behind Mama's house and hoot like an owl. Whenever Mama heard a hoot, she'd suddenly need to visit the outhouse. She'd run into Daddy's arms for a few stolen kisses, then rush back to the house before anyone missed her.

After several months of this, they decided to get married. There was no white dress, no wedding music, no bridal bouquet. Mama met Daddy at a friend's house, and they raced to the preacher's on horseback. Mama was 17 and Daddy 19. Mama's parents were livid at first, but Daddy eventually became their favorite son-in-law.

My parents were devoted and loving, both to each other and to their nine children. They allowed us to date early—though with supervision—and taught us to never judge people by anyone but themselves.

Postwar Shortage of Nylons Brought Couple into Line

By Frank Munkel, Fancy Gap, Virginia

AFTER World War II, there were still shortages of many commodities, including nylon stockings.

While shopping with my sister in Elizabeth, New Jersey, we stood in a long line outside a hosiery store that was selling one pair per person. I had a friend who was getting married soon and thought she'd appreciate an extra pair of nylons.

As we waited in the slow-moving line, my sister and I began talking with a young lady. After we all bought our nylons, my sister offered to drive our attractive new acquaintance home. I didn't mind. I got her telephone number before we dropped her off.

That was over 50 years ago, and my wife is still an exciting and loving individual. I don't believe too many fellows met their wives in nylon stocking lines.

Friday the 13th Proved Lucky for This Couple

By Beverly Allfree, Story City, Iowa

ONE FRIDAY the 13th in 1946, my brother and I arrived late for a football game at our school in Newton, Iowa. Our friends had already left our designated meeting place and there was no way to find them.

We found vacant seats next to a young man named Dick and started visiting with him. He'd just returned from the Navy and had enrolled at Newton High School to finish his class work and graduate.

That was the beginning of a whole new life for me. Dick and I began to date and continued dating after we graduated in 1948. We married in 1949 and have five children and four grandchildren. I've always been told that Friday the 13th is an unlucky day, but it sure wasn't for us!

Their 'Chance Meeting' Was an Answer to Prayer

*By Sharon Johnson
Hixson, Tennessee*

JERRY had been praying for a wife for several years. One day while reading the Bible, a verse seemed to leap out at him: "And the angel of the Lord found her by a fountain of water in the wilderness."

Jerry felt his prayers had been answered and that he'd meet his future wife at "the well"—his church. I joined that small church shortly afterward, and Jerry and I met, fell in love and married.

On the drive to our honeymoon chalet in Gatlinburg, Tennessee, we reminisced about the Bible verse and how we'd met at "the well". When we arrived at the chalet, we were amazed. Hanging above the staircase was a painting of a boy and girl at a well!

I tried to locate a print of this painting for several

WENT TO THE WELL. When Jerry was thirsting for a lifelong relationship, he turned to a higher power. He then met Sharon—no chance encounter.

years and even tried unsuccessfully to buy the copy from the chalet. Just before our ninth anniversary, I found a print of the painting in a craft store. I gave it to Jerry as an anniversary present.

The painting is called *Chance Meeting*. But I know without a doubt that ours was no chance meeting!

Ice Storm Stopped Trip But Started Romance

By Julie Fales
Mechanicsville, Virginia

I MET BILL in a college course. When he found out my name was Julie Snow, he asked if I knew Daniel Snow. I said I had an uncle by that name in Maryland. Bill looked surprised—and then told me my uncle was married to his aunt!

Then he asked me out for Saturday night, Valentine's Day. I told him I was going to Murphy, North Carolina with my friend, Sherri, but would call him if our plans changed.

STORM WAS OVER, and Bill and Julie were together. Their marriage and two daughters wouldn't exist today, had an ice storm not struck in North Carolina.

Friday afternoon, Sherri's mother called. There was a bad ice storm in Murphy, and she didn't want us traveling the treacherous roads. I called Bill and asked if his invitation still stood.

After our date, I told Sherri that Bill was the one. We've been married 9 years now and have two beautiful daughters.

Bill later told me he'd thought the trip to Murphy was an excuse to get out of the date. If I'd gone to Murphy that weekend, he wouldn't have asked me out again!

Some people believe in luck or fate. I believe in the Lord and His hand in our lives. Thank you, Lord, for everything—especially that ice storm.

Whirlwind Romance Began With a Last-Minute Date

By Charles Hendry
Silver Spring, Maryland

AT THE BEGINNING of World War II, I was stationed in Washington, D.C. Shortly after my arrival, a letter came from my mother.

A girl from my hometown was coming to Washington, and it would be neighborly of me to

THEY FACED OFF, at a hockey game that is, and Charles and Helen ended up married.

show her around. By the way, Mom added, this girl was 6 feet tall.

I'm 5-foot-8, but I knew a soldier who was 6 feet tall and even had a car. At a restaurant, the tall soldier and I discussed where to take the giantess. A hockey game would be ideal. "A hockey game," our waitress said. "Boy, I love hockey." We agreed to take her with us.

On the appointed date, we drove to the waitress' apartment, but her younger sister answered the door and didn't invite us in. She seemed flustered. It turned out an old boyfriend was in town, and the waitress had agreed to go out with him.

She said she hated to break up our foursome, but perhaps her sister Helen would like to go. The pretty young thing who'd greeted me at the door agreed, and we left to pick up the others.

The girl from my hometown was nice, but the waitress' younger sister was a delight. I saw her for the next 14 nights, and Helen and I were married several months later.

His Second Choice for Date
Was First Choice for Bride

By Glenda Beall, Hayesville, North Carolina

ONE SUMMER DAY in 1963, a young man named Barry called to invite my sister, Gay, to a picnic at the creek. He was new in town, and some mutual friends had suggested he call her. When Mother told him Gay wasn't home, he asked for me.

Barry sounded nice enough, but I was fresh out of college and a bad relationship, and I had sworn off boys. I was perfectly happy just riding my horse and catching up on my reading.

As we talked, I found out Barry had moved from California. That intrigued me. Then he said he'd pick me up in his convertible. I decided to take a chance.

The first part of the afternoon was miser-able. Barry ignored me while he played guitar and entertained the guests. The girls hung all over him, and it was obvious he enjoyed the attention. I longed to be home with my horse.

SECOND FIDDLE leapt to first, when Glenda Beall was home to take an unexpected phone call. She and Barry married in June, 1964.

After dark, Barry took me for a boat ride, and we talked under the stars for 2 hours. By the time he took me home, I was in love, and I believe he was, too. We got married the following June.

I've always been thankful Gay wasn't home that day. Sometimes being second choice is the best choice.

Getting off Subway for Walk Led to Life in New Country

By Doreen Astalos
Colonia, New Jersey

ONE January night in 1945, when I was 17, I spent the night at a friend's house in North London, England. The next day, during the long subway trip back to my house west of London, we decided to get off and walk to the next station.

As we crossed Piccadilly Circus, we saw two GI's coming toward us. They asked where we were going and whether they could come along. We said, "Sure, if you want a long train ride!" Seventeen stations later, we got off and walked to my house.

YOUNG YANKEE Andy Astalos posed for photo in Middlesex, England in April 1946.

My parents invited Andy and Lou in. I often brought GI's home to visit my family during the war. They were just homesick kids, and my folks always tried to make them feel at home. Dad liked Andy right away. "You're nuts if you let that one get away," he told me later.

Andy and I dated for 2 days in February, then again in April when he had a 7-day furlough. By then we were in love. He proposed on an island in the River Thames, and we planned to get married that July.

But when the war in Europe came to an end, Andy was shipped out to prepare for the invasion of Japan, and I didn't hear from him. I was heartbroken. I knew he lived in Linden, New Jersey, so I wrote to his mum. I didn't know she was Slavic and couldn't read or speak English.

When Andy was discharged in November, he finally wrote, said he still wanted to get married and offered to pay my fare to come to the US. It took a while for me to get there—war brides were sent first, and no one seemed to be very interested in the plight of anxious fiancees.

At last I arrived at Heathrow Airport, which had opened June 1, 1946. It was nothing more than a huge tent in a field with a single Pan Am plane standing there. After an 18-hour flight—we were grounded twice by bad weather—I landed at LaGuardia Airport and met Andy.

Andy and I were married June 30, 1946. We have four children and five grandchildren and are happily married still—all because my friend and I got off that subway for a little fresh air.

Spouses-to-Be Met Through Complex Set of Coincidences

By Wilda Richards, Lubbock, Texas

AFTER I graduated from college, my boyfriend talked me into taking a job in Columbia, Missouri where he was attending school. But a year later, he was in the service, and I was homesick. I decided to move home to Nevada, Missouri with my parents and younger sister.

My sister's husband was in the Coast Guard, and he was

DOMINOES OF FATE fell in just the right order for J.D. and Wilda. They were married May 7, 1945.

THESE DAYS, J.D. and Wilda enjoy retirement, three children and eight grandchildren.

coming home on leave. One of his shipmates happened to trade leaves with another fellow and accompanied him on the bus. When my sister and I went to the bus station to meet her husband, he had J.D. Richards with him.

J.D. had just broken up with someone, and I felt sorry for him, so I arranged a picnic lunch for the four of us. We saw each other on and off during that leave, dated on two leaves that followed and married May 7, 1945.

If I hadn't gone home when I did…if that other man hadn't traded leaves with J.D.…if I hadn't arranged the picnic that started our dating…we wouldn't have gotten together. But it all worked so perfectly that surely God arranged it!

Spoiled Girl's Disappointment Led to Lifetime of Blessings

By Emilie Cunningham, Durham, North Carolina

AS THE spoiled youngest child of a doctor, I planned to attend an affluent private college. I'd always managed to get what I wanted, so I was sure the college would be thrilled to have me.

Imagine my surprise when I received a letter of rejection. There'd been an error in transferring my grades, but by the time I found that out, the application deadline had passed. After a frantic search, my counselor found another school for me an hour from home, and I reluctantly enrolled.

In late September, a girl stopped by my room with a male friend and his dorm mate. The first boy was intended for me, but the other boy and I paired off immediately. It was love at first sight. We were engaged 8 months later and married the year we graduated.

Thirteen years and four sons later, I thank whomever rejected me from that elite school, and the counselor who pointed me in the right direction. What seemed like an inconvenient series of mishaps turned into many blessings.

Cheap Taxi Ride Changed the Course of Her Life

By Elizabeth Raymond
Seattle, Washington

SHE MISSED THE BUS but gained a husband! Elizabeth and Wilbert wed in 1946, thanks to her choice of transportation.

IN JANUARY 1946, I was on my way back to Coast Guard duty in Charleston, South Carolina after Christmas leave at home. My train got in late at night, and I headed for a bus to take me back to the barracks.

Suddenly a cab driver approached me. "I can take you back to the barracks for the same price you'd pay on the bus," he said. I climbed into the front seat and saw two sailors in back. Their ship, the *Buchanan*, was in Charleston to be decommissioned.

One of the sailors started a conversation with me and asked if I'd like to show him around Charleston. When we got to the barracks, I gave him my name and phone number. I thought, "Well, I'll probably never hear from him again." Wrong! Wilbert called the next day, and we went dancing at the USO.

We continued seeing each other until March, when I was sent home to Massachusetts. Wilbert was discharged soon after and returned to Seattle. We wrote to each other daily until August, when Wilbert drove cross-country with his parents and brother for our wedding.

THE RAYMONDS are all smiles today, wed 50 years and counting.

I often wonder where I would be today if I'd taken the bus back to the barracks instead of that taxi.

Sis the Matchmaker Struck a Spark

By Herbert Stearns, Windsor Locks, Connecticut

I FOUND the woman of my dreams...but not before I dated her sister!

The story starts when I was drafted into the army shortly after the Korean War broke out. I took my basic training at Ft. Devens, Massachusetts and finished in December 1950. I was given a 2-week furlough before being shipped overseas.

A buddy of mine was dating a girl in nearby Watertown, and he asked if I'd go on a double date with one of this girl's friends. I agreed.

Jean and I ended up going out on two dates, after which she told her sister she thought I was better suited to her. That was fine with me, so I began dating Doris.

After our second night out, I knew this was the girl I wanted to marry. Though I'd only known her a few days, I

asked Doris to wait for me. She did!

I was shipped to Korea with the Signal Corps in January 1951 and remained there until September, 1952. During that time, we wrote each other faithfully.

We got together after my discharge from the Army and were married in 1954. We've enjoyed 40-plus wonderful years and owe it all to her sister.

Thanks, Jean!

SAVVY SISTER made it possible for Doris and Herbert to meet. This photo was taken in 1955.

Cupid Was an 11-Year-Old

By Twyla Gilkey Isett, Inverness, Florida

I'D BEEN widowed for several years when I learned that my 11-year-old son missed his father more than I realized.

The year was 1948, and we'd recently moved to Columbus Juction, Iowa. One day, Lynn mentioned he needed a new bulb for his bed lamp and asked permission to ride his bicycle the few blocks to the hardware store. He'd never ventured that far before, but it was a small town, so I consented.

When he didn't return as promptly as I'd expected, I called the store. A pleasant-sounding man assured me that yes, Lynn had been there and was on his way home. I noted a bit of a chuckle in the man's voice...I'd learn the reason for that later.

In about 10 days, a handwritten letter arrived in my mailbox. It was from the hardware store clerk, William Gilkey.

He politely introduced himself and said that although he did not know me, he would be delighted to take me to the auto races next Saturday.

To say I was puzzled would be an understatement. Not only did I not know this man, I didn't even like car racing. What was going on?

I took the letter to my aunt and uncle, who were longtime

residents of Columbus Junction. Did they know him?

They laughed heartily and said of course they knew him. He was a fine man who'd raised his three children alone. Everyone who knew William liked him.

"Why don't you go," my uncle encouraged. "It might be fun." I was tempted...but hesitant.

A week later, Lynn said, "Mom, you didn't even answer that letter, and I hoped you would! I met that guy, and I liked him, so I asked him to take you out."

That explained what was going on. But persistent little Lynn wasn't quite finished. Undaunted by my unresponsiveness, he'd again invited the man to meet me.

"He's coming by tonight," Lynn announced. "He's going to ask if it's okay to ride along with us next Sunday when you drive me to Cub Scout camp. You know how you don't like to drive home alone on that road through the swamp."

Well, he came...and we went...and liked each other.

Our friendship quickly blossomed into love, and 6 months later, we were married.

I gained a wonderful husband, he found the joy of a home where his grown children would feel welcome all the rest of their lives, and my son was very happy to have a new daddy.

All because my little lad decided to play cupid.

After 60 Years, He Finally Won 'the Girl Across the Aisle'

By Glenn Gish, Mechanicsburg, Pennsylvania

IN 1926, I was a teenager attending a one-room country schoolhouse near Millersburg, Pennsylvania.

One evening, the teacher put on a play, and two cousins and I sang a song called *The Girl Across the Aisle*. It began like this: "When the teacher isn't looking, I just rest my eyes a spell on a little girl who isn't far away..."

For me, Frances was the girl across the aisle. But anoth-

ACROSS THE AISLE no more, Glenn and Frances are together forever.

er fellow in our class got a car before I did, and he beat me to Frances. They got married, and later on, I did, too. Frances and I went our separate ways for over 60 years.

When my wife died of cancer, I was alone and decided to stay that way. No one wants an 80-year-old man anyway, and I had to decide what to do with the rest of my life.

One day, Frances came to mind, but I didn't think much about her then. I didn't even know if she was still alive. It wasn't long before she was on my mind every day.

I told my son about Frances, and said I wanted to find her. I was in Austin, Texas, and as far as I knew, she was 1,600 miles away in Pennsylvania. He bought me plane tickets for my birthday in June 1993.

Finding Frances was easy. My brother knew she lived in a retirement village, and she'd been alone for 30 years.

I figured if she'd wanted to remarry, she would have done so long ago. If I called or wrote, she might say she wasn't interested. So I just showed up at her door.

Frances invited me in, and we talked about old times for awhile. Then I said, "You know why I'm really here? I came to take you back to Texas with me." She threw up her hands and said, "Never!"

But we kept talking, and I told her I wanted to go back to the area where we'd attended school. She thought that was a great idea and agreed to go along a few days later.

That first day together, we had lunch at the village cafeteria. About halfway through my meal, I put down my fork. "This has never happened to me before," I told Frances. "I can't finish my meal." I had butterflies in my stomach! She said she had the same problem.

During my 2 weeks in Pennsylvania, I visited Frances as often as I could. I enjoyed her company, and I loved her. Near the end of my vacation, I asked her to marry me. She said yes!

Chapter Seven

Their Love Changed My Life

Encouragement Turned Timid Bride into Capable Woman

By Helen Smith, Alton, Illinois

MY HUSBAND, Dale, and I grew up in neighboring country towns in Missouri. Our mothers carpooled to work together, and his father drove my school bus. But we didn't really know each other until his mother suggested I start writing him.

Dale was 4 years older, serving in the Navy and was getting discouraged because no one wrote him except his parents. I agreed to write. That first letter turned into several more and then some dates when he came home on leave.

There were many more letters and then marriage when he returned home in 1954. I was a very timid bride and had little confidence in myself.

Dale went to work for the Army Corps of Engineers and often heard his coworkers say their wives couldn't handle the simplest household repairs or even put gas in the car. He also knew two widows who'd had a terrible time because their husbands hadn't told them anything about repairs, insurance, deeds or finances.

Dale didn't want anything like that to happen to me. If anything ever happened to him, he wanted

YOU CAN DO IT! Dale Smith, seen here with Helen during early '70s, was encouraging.

me to be able to take care of myself and the kids. He began teaching me things he thought I should know.

I learned how to put oil in my car and check it. I learned simple carpentry, how to service the lawn mower and how to replace a bulb socket in a lamp. Most importantly, Dale made sure I knew all about our finances.

When I got interested in crafts, I sometimes became frustrated when the instructions weren't clear. Dale would say, "Come on, let's see what we can do." In a few minutes, he'd have it figured out, and I'd be able to finish my project.

Through the years, he kept encouraging me to try more things. As I gained confidence, I realized I was capable of much more than I'd thought.

I became active in the Mother's Club at our children's school, joined the church choir and became president of the church's Dorcas Circle—things I wouldn't have even considered in earlier years. And it was all because my husband believed in me.

In 1987, Dale passed away at age 55. Because of his encouragement and his confidence in me, I've been able to make a lot of tough decisions on my own. God was sure good to me, letting me have 33 years with this wonderful man.

Santa's Magic Opened Her Eyes to Stepfather's Love

By Yvonne Tymoczko, Bucksport, Maine

I WAS 1-1/2 years old when my father died. My mother remarried 2 years later, on Election Day in November.

I don't remember the wedding, but I remember walking into my new father's house and starting to cry because I didn't like the furniture.

That was only the beginning. My hostility continued, much to my new father's sorrow.

On Christmas Eve, my uncle came to the house dressed up as Santa Claus. I was frightened by Santa. I looked at Mom, sitting on one side of the room. Then I looked at my new father, sitting across from her. When I ran to him and put my arms around his neck, tears streamed down his face.

I have always thought Santa was something like magic. Well, he sure was for me. He helped me find the real love that my new father felt for me.

Stand-in Godfather Met
Future Wife at the Altar

By Marie Radeck, Silver Bay, Minnesota

IN 1881, a young soldier named John Stammen was assigned to take some prisoners from Montana to Fort Snelling, Minnesota.

Afterward, while on furlough, he visited a church in St. Paul. A baby was to be baptized that day, but the godfather hadn't shown up. John was asked to stand in with the godmother, a shy young woman named Helen.

After the ceremony, the child's family invited John to dinner, where he and Helen felt a mutual attraction. When he returned to the Army, they began to write. Over the next 2 years, their friendship blossomed into love.

John and Helen married in June 1883, 1 month after his discharge, and were blessed with three daughters. John wrote in his autobiography that their marriage was "a bed of roses".

It seems this union was made in heaven; it surely began in church. The shy young lady and the nice young soldier were my grandparents.

So their love did more than change my life. It made my life possible.

CAPABLE STAND-IN. John and Helen Stammen were married June 21, 1883 —thanks to a missing godfather.

Boyfriend's Quick Action May Have Saved Her

By Christina Frizzell, North Adams, Michigan

WHEN I was in eighth grade, a new boy moved to town. I knew there was something special about him the minute I saw him, and we became good friends. In our sophomore year, we began to date.

The following summer, I was driving to pick up my younger sister and passed the place where my boyfriend worked. A few seconds later, I lost control of my car. It flipped onto its side and slammed into a tree, flattening the roof.

My boyfriend was one of the first people on the scene and kept me awake while the ambulance was on its way. I was later told that his

ON THE SPOT was Christina's reliable boyfriend. As her husband, he remains reliable.

action may have kept me from slipping into a coma.

We are now married and have a son. I often think about that accident and know that if my husband hadn't been there, I might not be here today.

Saintly Husband Remained Devoted to the End

By Nan Householder, Toronto, Ohio

WHEN I was 17 and a senior in high school, a friend and I went to a carnival, where she introduced me to her cousin. This wonderful guy became my husband of 48 years.

Eugene had been to World War II and back and was ready

to settle down. He would do anything to make me happy, and that wasn't always easy. We were married in 1947.

Our first child was a girl—followed by three more girls. Eugene was his parents' only son, and we hoped for a boy to carry on the family name.

But Eugene was never disappointed when the doctor said, "Another girl". He'd just laugh and say, "Now I have one more girl to love." Eventually our prayers were answered, and we were blessed with a son. How thankful we both were.

Gladly Accepted Responsibility

After my mother's early death, we took in my sister and two brothers so they could finish school. Not once did Eugene complain about this added responsibility.

We didn't have city water at the time, so Eugene took all the laundry to work with him and went to the laundromat when his shift was over. What a help that was to me. I didn't have a driver's license, so Eugene also did most of the shopping and drove the kids to all their activities.

Eugene loved to fish, and once a year he'd take all of us and a cousin to Canada. As I look back, that was no vacation for him—but what great memories for the kids and me.

After the girls married, Eugene wanted to build a new house for us to retire in. I was very happy with the big old house we had, but he deserved his dream house. He worked at the plant for 42 years, drove a bus, drove a truck—anything to help out. He even saved for a nice big boat so we could fish and take it easy once he retired.

But it was not in the cards. Eugene spent the last 10 years of his life with Parkinson's disease and Alzheimer's. He spent his last 2 years in a nursing home. Some days he didn't recognize me.

One day at the home, he was restless, and the nurse gave him a pen and paper. He hadn't been able to write for some time, but when I went to visit him that day, the nurse gave me the paper. Eugene had written, "Nan, I love you." I will treasure it forever.

If I hadn't gone to that carnival so many years ago, I may never have met the best man in the world. His love changed my life in so many positive ways.

Chapter Eight

The Stranger
Who Helped
Me Most

Papers from This Train Opened Worlds To Farm Girl

By Lee Hill-Nelson
Waco, Texas

THE KINDNESS of a railroad man opened up a larger world to me, a country girl—a world that helped me to read, laugh and dream.

In the 1930s, Papa moved our family of nine from Bridle Bit to Buffalo Flat, both near Turkey, Texas. Something exciting happened in Buffalo Flat.

LOVED FUNNY PAPERS. Lee Hill-Nelson, at age 12, was recipient of a stranger's kindness on an unusual paper route.

Every evening, out of the west, what looked like a huge black doodlebug came speeding down the train tracks about a block from our house. The little train had an engine, a passenger car, a dining car and a baggage car.

Life was quiet in the country. I'd stare at the dressed-up people on the train and imagine stories about them—happy people traveling to faraway places. Maybe they were rich.

Became Fan of the Funnies

I watched for the doodlebug every night, and from down the track a way, I'd hear the whistle blow. In the door stood a man waving a rolled-up newspaper.

As the train passed our house, the man would throw down the paper—usually a day-old *Denver Post*, sometimes the *Fort Worth Star-Telegram*. My sister or I would run to the tracks to retrieve it.

Adventures began with Little Orphan Annie, Mary Worth, Dick Tracy and Dixie Dugan, an attorney with a short hairdo and bangs. I wanted to look like Dixie when I grew up.

One day, the doodlebug stopped for repairs. The man in the black uniform got off, waved a newspaper and motioned for me to come down to the tracks. I'd never been close to a train.

"Hello," he said, reaching to shake my hand. "My name's Tom Huggins." I stared at him, knowing I was supposed to say something. No sounds came out. I looked down at my dirty bare feet, hoping he didn't see them. I took the newspaper and ran home.

When I entered high school, the newspapers continued to teach me about life in a bigger world. Perhaps someday I'd live in Denver or Fort Worth.

Then World War II began. Patriotism and the heartache of war reached our farm through the newspapers.

All Aboard!

After I graduated from high school, my sister and I moved to Dallas to work. Some months later, going home for a visit, we rode the doodlebug from Childress to Turkey.

Excitement filled me from my toes to the top of my head when I saw Mr. Huggins collecting tickets. We told him who we were and where we were headed.

"I'm glad you're riding this train," he said. As he shook our hands, a big smile crossed his face. "I threw you newspapers for years." Surely we were in the company of an old friend.

Dusk had set in when we passed our house. Mama was on the front porch. The engineer blew his whistle. With a flashlight in one hand, Mr. Huggins waved a newspaper and threw it to Mama. On it, he had written: "Meet your daughters at the train station. They're coming home."

That was my only ride on the doodlebug. Folks just quit riding trains, and now the doodlebug is no more.

Thank you, Mr. Huggins, wherever you are. Because you cared and took the time to wave your newspapers, you enriched a young girl's life.

Boss' Confidence Gave
Her Faith in Herself

By Mrs. Thurlie Fish, Vacaville, California

MANY PEOPLE experience a turning point that changes their lives. Mine came in 1950, when I was working for a bank.

I was just 19, an insecure brand-new secretary. Most of my work came from the treasurer, Mr. Cubberley. He moved like a freight train from chore to chore, barely stopping anywhere long enough to make his wishes clear—especially to an inexperienced teenager.

One day, Mr. Cubberley blew past and dropped a 2-inch stack of securities on my desk. "Send these to Merrill Lynch, Pierce, Fenner and Bean in New York," he said. "You'll find a form in your desk there somewhere. I want triplicate copies."

I was just a country girl. I'd never seen securities before, let alone the form in my desk. But fear of looking stupid sealed my lips. I'd find it.

I did, and it looked fairly simple. I neatly tucked three carbons between the sheets and coaxed my typewriter into accepting the bulk.

She'd Figure It Out

Respecting my inexperience, Mr. Cubberley had included a sheet listing the number of shares on each certificate, along with the first couple of words in each title. I could figure out the rest.

Mr. Cubberley was known for his horrible penmanship, but by the second or third certificate, I was off and running. Piece of cake.

When I finished, the pages were neat as a pin. But just to be sure, I double checked everything carefully. Then I noticed something curious—every certificate ended in an "8"— 38 shares, 18 shares, 108 shares.

I checked the securities themselves. And then I panicked. Every listing I had typed was wrong. Mr. Cubberley's script always ran together, and each "8" was actually the initial "S", meaning "shares".

I had to do it all over—and I'd already spent too much time on this assignment. I ripped off a new set of forms and carefully but hurriedly retyped the entire list.

When I reluctantly took the papers to Mr. Cubberley, he pointed to them and asked, "Do you think this is right?"

"I think they're right," I stammered.

"That's good enough for me," he declared, whipping to the last page and

THOROUGHLY CAPABLE was Thurlie Fish, a young secretary who needed some reassurance to learn that.

scrawling his illegible signature. Then he handed me the stack, pointed to the postage meter and said, "Send it. You'll find envelopes underneath. Insure it for $200,000." Just like that! No checking, no hassles, no reprisals. I was in shock.

Mr. Cubberley changed my life that day. If he could put that much trust in me, maybe I did have worth after all. He'll never know how much he boosted my wavering self-esteem with that simple act of faith.

I wish everyone could find their own Mr. Cubberley. If not, then try to *be* one. It's the next best thing.

Heroic Eagle Scout Saved Drowning Boy

By Robert DeBuhr
Rainier, Oregon

HE'S PREPARED. This scout wears uniform common in the days when author's life was saved.

IN 1930 when I was 10 years old, I was playing in the Columbia River just west of Longview, Washington. I accidentally stepped off into the ship channel, and the undertow swept me downstream. I couldn't swim.

The mothers who'd brought us to the beach were helpless to save me, but their frantic screams were heard a quarter-mile away by a 16-year-old Eagle Scout.

Leonard Hanley raced down the beach, stripping off most of his clothes, and plunged into the river. By then, I had gone under for the last time and had lost consciousness.

Leonard dove and pulled me to the surface. Another man helped pull me into a rowboat. Leonard climbed in after me and began performing an early type of CPR.

When we reached shore, Leonard continued doing rescue breathing until I regained consciousness. Someone carried me to a houseboat, where I was placed between clean white sheets. My rescuer had vanished.

My folks were finally able to locate Leonard, and he became my idol. He was one of only seven people that year to be awarded the Carnegie Medal for bravery. He went on to become an honor student, president of his high school class and captain of the state-championship football team.

I became a Boy Scout, grew up to be a Scoutmaster and spent 30 years as a professional Scout executive. By saving my life, Leonard made it possible for many more boys to grow up in his image, including my own Eagle Scout son.

Teacher's Legacy of Generosity Now Touches Another Generation

By Mary Meek, Wheeling, West Virginia

I GREW UP in West Alexander, Pennsylvania and worked as a waitress to help my parents put me through college. When my father had a tractor accident one summer, I vowed to keep working and put myself through school.

One day, an "old maid" schoolteacher named Miss Moss called me to her home and asked how much money I needed to go to school that fall. I told her I planned to keep working, but she wouldn't hear of it.

Miss Moss insisted on giving me the money and sent me home with strict orders to talk to my mother about it. Mom suggested I visit the bank to see if they could tell me anything about Miss Moss.

The banker told me to take the money. He said I would never know how many young people Miss Moss had helped. I couldn't believe it. She didn't even have a TV!

Mom and I had a meeting with Miss Moss, and we all shared a good cry as the financial arrange-

SUCCESS. Mary's 1966 graduation photo might not have been snapped, if not for a stranger.

ments were made. When I graduated, it was imperative that Miss Moss attend. She had kept me in school.

After Miss Moss died, I attended her estate auction. I wanted to buy something of hers to continue the bond we'd shared. While there, I found her retirement records. She had been making $6,400 a year.

When I told my husband about this wonderful woman, we agreed to continue Miss Moss' tradition and help some children through college ourselves. Some parents have been shocked by our offer, but it all started with this generous old maid schoolteacher in West Alexander.

Mysterious Writer Changed Paraplegic Teenager's Life

By Antoinette Capek
Lemont, Illinois

A CLASS MEMBER, though at home, was Antoinette in 1941.

"YBF" was someone I would never meet. This person first wrote to me in 1942, when I was 14 years old and living on a farm near Cornell, Wisconsin.

Dear Antoinette,

The pages from the Wisconsin Agricultural and Farmer *magazine were used to protect and pack machine parts sent to the department where I work. I noticed your picture in the Women's Department written by Lois Hurley. She wrote of your physical handicap and 4-H achievement. Due to your inability to travel, I will attempt to make you an armchair traveler. We will travel by picture postcards throughout New England's scenic sights.* —YBF

Who was YBF? And why would a stranger be interested in anyone so many miles away, much less a teenage paraplegic?

The next day, my postcard tour began. A "view card" came to our rural roadside mailbox every day, depicting a historical site or landmark from Maine to Virginia.

Each card carried a small notation regarding the scene and the "YBF" signature. If a holiday interrupted mail delivery, there were two cards in the box the next day.

As the months passed, I never learned any details of YBF's personal life. I didn't even know if my friend was male or female.

"YBF must be a retired schoolteacher," Mom said, as she brought in the mail one afternoon. "Only a teacher would write so beautifully." Each letter was perfectly formed, each line neat and consistent.

"YBF stands for 'your boyfriend'," my aunt remarked after reading a few of the cards.

At the end of one year, a letter arrived.

> *Dear Antoinette,*
> *I hope you enjoyed being an armchair traveler. I have tried to send picture postcards of sites you may have studied, plus many scenes you might enjoy as I do, while I escorted you around our beautiful country. I hope you have found this type of traveling enjoyable.*
> *You should receive a package in a few days. I am sending you some materials you may find of value and entertaining.* —*Your Boston Friend*
> *Charles F. Higgins*

Your Boston Friend! At last we knew the meaning of those initials.

"You got a package! You got a package!" my 3-year-old sister Charlotte shouted a few days later. Mother brought in a large elongated box and placed it on the tray attached to my wheelchair.

COLORFUL POSTCARDS brightened Antoinette's life, thanks to a mysterious correspondent, "YBF".

776 *Dianthus caryophyllus L.* - *Garten-Nelke*
Oeillet des fleuristes - Garofano - Garden Pink

So glad you enjoy these flower cards. With your love for flowers, I knew you would have great success making the paper ones, as you could put in that little touch that would be lacking, when done by a person that just makes them for a hobby.

Y. B. F.

"Open it!" Charlotte cried. "Open it!" I quickly tore off the binding tape and pulled back the flaps. Inside the box were folds of brightly colored crepe paper, wires, paste, stamens and a book, *How to Make Crepe Paper Flowers*.

I suppose you often wonder why I enjoy sending these little things to you. I think you will find the answer in the last verse of this poem, that I have underscored:

Do Something For Somebody Else

The world is encumbered with sorrow and care—
With longing for happiness every where;
If then, you would lighten the burdens of life
And lessen its toil and its worry and strife —
Do something for somebody else.

We rush madly on in our daily careers,
And each takes his measure of smiles and of tears;
We flippantly mingle the bad and the good
Nor seemingly care for the fact that we should
Do something for somebody else.

Each plays his small part in Life's feverish game;
And scrambles for honors and riches and fame;
Grows selfish and craven and full of distrust;
Yet, if we would truly be happy, we must
Do something for somebody else.

Oh, you who are full of complaining and fears,
Who think but of Self through the slow moving years;
Pray, let me prescribe for Life's fevers and chills,
Its mental and moral and physical ills;
Do Something For Somebody Else.

Do something for somebody else and forget
Your own petty troubles. Why worry and fret?
Let Love in your heart be forever enshrined:
He lives most who gives most of self to mankind
Do something for somebody else.

"No candy?" a disappointed Charlotte asked.

"No candy," I said, cheerfully sorting through the folds of paper. I quickly depleted the contents of the box, making carnations, daisies, peonies, roses, lilies, tulips and other flowers.

I found myself ordering more flower-making supplies as I began making bouquets for gifts. Soon I

MYSTERY REVEALED! Antoinette finally put a face with a name when Charles F. Higgins (upper right corner) sent this 1947 photo of his son's wedding party.

had orders from relatives, friends, and friends of friends. I continued making crepe paper flowers for years.

When we moved to Chicago in 1946, I switched to chenille, making poinsettias for the women who worked with Mom. That provided extra money for a photo-coloring course. I tinted black-and-white photos with oil paint until color prints became less expensive.

Charles F. Higgins, while raising nine children of his own, somehow found time to bring new challenges into my life. He not only led me to an interesting and profitable hobby, but helped me realize that I should use the abilities I had, rather than dwelling on what I didn't have. We remained pen pals until 1948.

Today, I make my flowers on a computer screen to decorate greeting cards and letters. And I still travel with postcards via friends, who adopted Mr. Higgins' idea.

If Charles F. Higgins happens to read this, I want him and his family to know that his thoughtfulness and generosity were not wasted, nor will they ever be forgotten. I felt truly blessed to have him for a friend.

In one of his letters to me, Mr. Higgins explained the reason why he was being so generous with his time and attention: